CHAIRMAN'S NOTE

ALEXANDER S. FRIEDMAN

Project Syndicate's 2019 year-ahead magazine, *The Great Disruption*, is a critically important collection of commentaries and insights for this dangerous moment in human history. A century after the end of World War I, there are many worrying similarities between our own era and the period around 1918, when a wave of nationalism reshaped Europe.

The November 1918 Armistice proved to be a false dawn. The political and economic turmoil of that era would continue for decades, until the Western powers emerged victorious from World War II. They committed to building a new global order, and laid the foundation for the development of the United Nations, the European Union, the International Monetary Fund, the World Bank, the North Atlantic Treaty Organization, and the General Agreement on Tariffs and Trade (the precursor to the World Trade Organization). With the United States playing a leading and stabilizing role, this multilateral framework succeeded in integrating the global economy, lifting billions of people out of poverty, and preventing another world war.

Yet human lives are relatively short, and humanity's collective memory may be only slightly longer. Today, many of the self-styled "disruptive" leaders in Europe, Asia, and the Americas see an opportunity for political gain in condemning the very structures that enabled their rise. With fewer voters who remember the atrocities that made those structures necessary in the first place, populists can present nationalism, racism, and cults of personality as an attractive new kind of politics for the marginalized and the disaffected.

If Thucydides were alive today, he would advise us to study our history carefully. As he well knew, we humans drive our own fate, and we can easily repeat the tragic mistakes of the past. Whether one looks to the early twentieth century or to the Peloponnesian War between Athens and Sparta in the fourth century BC, greed and lust for power, unconstrained by impersonal rules and institutions, have long produced catastrophic results.

And yet, just as we are prone to repeat past mistakes, we can replicate past successes. We can stand against demagoguery, xenophobia, and fear, as many of our predecessors have done. But to succeed, we must protect the truth and facts, while also tolerating – indeed welcoming – the views of those who see things differently than we do.

To that end, *Project Syndicate* represents a unique social good. It is the only platform that enables the leading thinkers of our time to share their opinions with audiences around the world. There has never been a more important moment to cherish and support such a resource.

Thank you for helping to ensure that diverse and deeply informed perspectives on our world and its most pressing challenges continue to be heard. PS

Alexander S. Friedman is Chairman of Project Syndicate's advisory board.

The
New
Abnormal

THINK

For a disruptive approach to economic and financial analysis visit **ing.com/THINK**

ADVISORY BOARD MEMBER'S NOTE

MARK CLIFFE

Mainstream economists might dismiss as hyperbole the notion that we are in the midst of a Great Disruption. Judged solely by macroeconomic data, the world is not in bad shape. Growth, while mixed, shows no sign of tipping into recession; and with inflation fairly subdued, central banks are in no hurry to raise interest rates.

But to focus on such indicators is to miss the fact that macroeconomics is inherently political. Different people experience the economy in different ways. And by voting, citizens can reshape policy, and hence economic performance. Moreover, politics is not just about economics – indeed, populism is on the rise despite generally healthy macroeconomic indicators.

The political polarization that is a defining feature of the Great Disruption reflects the polarization of people, profits, and the planet. These are the three Ps of corporate-sustainability advocates' "triple bottom line," and, as matters stand, companies are generally finding themselves at the pole opposite to the populists.

The polarization of people reflects the growing perception that the benefits of globalization and new technology are not being shared fairly. Identity politics has thrived on the resulting divisions between rich and poor, old and young, and urban and rural. The wedge between groups has been widened by the rise of social media, which has enabled the emergence of echo chambers of extreme views and empowered purveyors of disinformation.

More broadly, disruptive digital technology is also a factor in the polarity of profits, fueling a growing divide between the haves and the have-nots. Its inflation of aggregate profits in a way that disproportionately benefits the rich has been amplified by the inflation of stock-market valuations on the back of unprecedented asset purchases by major central banks. And within the corporate sector, incumbents in a growing range of sectors are also wrestling with the rise of Big Tech, and its rapid growth through network effects and increasing returns to scale.

Meanwhile, the struggle for technological dominance between the US and China is polarizing the planet. The election of US President Donald Trump and other populists is fraying the bonds of international cooperation. The direct economic impact of the Trump administration's "America First" trade policy is yet to be fully realized, as is the effect of Brexit and resurgent populism on the European Union.

With the world having only just begun to contemplate the indirect effects of frayed relations in other domains such as security, migration, and climate advocacy, mainstream economists may want to take the Great Disruption seriously after all. PS

Mark Cliffe, *Chief Economist and Head of Global Research of the ING Group, is a member of Project Syndicate's advisory board.*

The Year Ahead 2019

Project Syndicate

Advisory Board

Bertrand Badré
Gordon Brown
Mark Cliffe
Gene Frieda
Alexander Friedman
Chair
Mike Hanley

Editorial Board

Roman Frydman
Kenneth Murphy
Editor in Chief
Andrzej Rapaczynski
Jonathan Stein
Managing Editor
Stuart Whatley
Deputy Editor

Editors

Whitney Arana
Associate Editor
Greg Bruno
Associate Editor
Rachel Danna
Assistant Managing Editor
Splinter Knight
Digital Editor
Jason Linback
Special Projects Editor

Contributing Editors

Anatole Kaletsky
Nina L. Khrushcheva
Joanna Rose
Laurence Tubiana

Publishing

Marissa Baard
Distribution & Translation Manager
Kasia Broussalian
Audience Engagement Manager
Nicolas Chatara-Morse
Chief Executive Officer
Damen Dowse
Vice President of Development
Jonathan Hoffmann
Chief Operating Officer
Jovana Jovic
Publishing Data & Analysis Manager
Peter Kupček
Chief Financial Officer
Carmen Morejón
Publishing Data Analyst
Petra Nemcekova
Data Analyst
Zuzana Pavlíková
Office Manager
Lindsey Pollard
Digital Sales & Marketing Associate
Callum Voge
Senior Global Relations Manager
Anna West
Social Media & Communications Associate
Nikita Wong
Assistant Distribution & Translation Manager

Designed by Texture
www.studiotexture.co.uk

© Project Syndicate 2019

Europe Writ How Large?

PS. Interview

Trump's Tariff Tantrum

Regulating the Revolution

Meeting the Challenge

EDITORS' INTRODUCTION

THE GREAT DISRUPTION

First came the Great Depression, which paved the road to World War II, and later served as an impetus for the creation of the liberal international order. Then came the "Great Moderation," an extended period of low volatility, starting in the mid-1980s, that bred complacency across the advanced economies. And then came the Great Recession, a severe economic downturn that coincided with and accelerated a broader political, economic, and social reckoning: the Great Disruption.

The Great Disruption is discernible not just in the widespread political backlash against the established world order, but also in the realm of technology, which is advancing faster than existing governance systems' ability to manage the effects. It is evident in the rebalancing of economic and geopolitical power away from the transatlantic region and toward the Asia-Pacific region, and in the emergence – in China and elsewhere – of new state-led economic-development models. It is a force that has transcended mere human affairs and manifested itself in nature, through rising tides, violent hurricanes, wildfires, and droughts. Images of the Great Disruption are ubiquitous, and they are multiplied and amplified by the digital platforms that have come to mediate the public sphere.

In the following pages, some of the world's leading thinkers and policymakers consider how these issues shaped global affairs in 2018, and their likely impact in the year ahead. We cannot yet know if the Great Disruption represents an episode of historical "creative destruction" or a more permanent reversal of fortune. But without a concerted effort to understand it, we can neither harness its benefits nor manage its costs.

The Politics of Disruption

If there were a dictum for our age, it might well be Antonio Gramsci's observation that when "the old is dying and the new cannot be born…morbid phenomena of the most varied kind come to pass." Less cited are Gramsci's warnings about the reconstitution of traditional political parties around "incoherent and muddled ideologies that feed on sentiments and emotion," and the tendency of disconsolate classes to "attach themselves to the glories of the past as a shield against the future." Whether one looks to Donald Trump in the United States, Jair Bolsonaro in Brazil, or Great Britain's Brexiteers, Gramsci's description certainly seems to fit the prevailing politics of the Great Disruption.

Starting with Trump, Nobel laureate economist Joseph E. Stiglitz examines both the economics and the politics of the US president's policies to "make America great again." Stiglitz concludes that the massive corporate tax cuts Trump signed into law in December 2017 have done nothing but enrich the already wealthy at the expense of "the majority of Americans in the middle of the income distribution." In 2018, Trump launched his long-awaited trade war, and continued to crack down on economically beneficial immigration. But perhaps worst of all, "Trump's brand of racism, misogyny, and nationalist incitement," Stiglitz writes, "has established franchises in Brazil, Hungary, Italy, Turkey, and elsewhere."

Still, how best to categorize the politics of the Great Disruption remains up for debate. For his part, British historian Michael Burleigh pushes back against the popular notion that Trump and his compatriots are latter-day "fascists." A more accurate parallel, he argues, is to the traditional right "before and after World War I," when conservatism "became infected by authoritarian and corporatist ideas, as well as a hatred of the left, Jews, and teeming cosmopolitan metropolises such as Berlin, Madrid, and Vienna."

Sebastián Edwards of UCLA offers still another parallel, namely, to Latin American populists in the mold of the late Hugo Chávez. Edwards sees "many similarities between Latin America's experience with populism and that of the advanced economies today," from mounting fiscal deficits to the manner in which Western populists "actually conduct politics." One key difference, he notes, is that older democracies have more developed systems of checks and balances. If those should fail, then lower- and middle-class voters, like their counterparts in Latin America, may "find themselves worse off than they were when the populist experiment was launched."

Ivan Krastev, Chairman of the Center for Liberal Strategies in Sofia, shows that in Central Europe's nativist turn, history and psychology also loom large. "The post-1989 settlement," he notes, "created a festering sense of resentment." And now, after three decades of being told to "Imitate the West," Poles, Hungarians, and other Central Europeans have grown tired of being "dominated by feelings of inadequacy, inferiority, dependency, and lost identity."

On a brighter note, Anwar Ibrahim, Malaysia's long-imprisoned opposition leader, helped to oust the party that had controlled his country since independence, reminding us that political disruption need not take the form of recrudescent populism or nationalism. As 2018 began, Anwar was behind bars on trumped-up charges; now he is helping lead an ambitious reform effort to establish Malaysia as a model democracy.

Here, he explains how that change emerged from a combination of traditional politicking and transcendent acts of forgiveness, in the process showing how pluralism, equality, and grace can still win out over chauvinism and fear.

A World Adrift

In 2018, the geostrategic shift away from the North Atlantic gained steam, owing in no small measure to actions taken by the Trump administration. To former British Prime Minister Gordon Brown, Trump's "America First" agenda represents the exact opposite of what is needed now. The world is even less prepared for an economic downturn than it was in the dark days of 2008, and Trump's unnecessary disputes with friends and foes alike are making cross-border collaboration increasingly difficult. "Whether the issue is financial stability, climate change, or tax havens," Brown reminds us that "national interests are best served through international cooperation."

Unfortunately, Trump's routine attacks on NATO and the EU are having real-world effects, both on the US's bipartisan commitment to its transatlantic alliances, and on those alliances' ability to confront emerging threats. To Julianne Smith, who was a deputy national security adviser to former US Vice President Joe Biden, Trump's intent is clear: "He is divesting America's holdings in the transatlantic relationship, and abandoning America's traditional leadership role both on the world stage and within institutions like NATO."

Likewise, former Israeli Foreign Minister Shlomo Ben-Ami sees the "Trump doctrine" as an explicit effort to abandon "America's longstanding role as a global arbiter." In 2018, the implications of this doctrine were on full display, particularly in the Middle East, where the US has been exacerbating conflicts and pushing strategically important countries closer toward Russia. But to Ben-Ami, the most worrying development of all is Trump's scrapping of the Iran nuclear deal, the dangers of which "cannot be overstated." ➡

1:
DONALD TRUMP AND VLADIMIR PUTIN.

Nonetheless, while Trump has been escalating tensions with Iran, he has been pursuing unprecedentedly high-level diplomacy with North Korea to wind down that country's nuclear program. Former South Korean foreign minister Yoon Young-kwan is happy to report that "fears of a military conflict on the Korean Peninsula have subsided" since late 2017, when Trump was threatening "fire and fury." Looking ahead, though, Yoon concludes that further progress will depend on whether the Trump administration can offer the security guarantees that the North Korean regime has long sought. If not, the international community may find that it has missed a historic opportunity.

Europe Writ How Large?

The Great Disruption has served as a wake-up call for governments around the world, but nowhere more than in Europe. Most Europeans now recognize that they can no longer rely fully on the US for their economic and military security. Yet how best to secure European sovereignty in an increasingly multipolar world is up for debate. European integration has stalled, but so has European *disintegration*, with the United Kingdom's withdrawal from the EU rapidly going from tragedy to farce. Which direction the Union takes hinges on the outcome of the European Parliament election in May 2019, and pro-integration forces are at risk of losing the upper hand.

With this in mind, European Commission President Jean-Claude Juncker emphasizes the fact that, "Individual European countries simply do not have the clout to shape global affairs on their own, and that is not going to change." As such, they must get behind a "more united and democratic" EU if they are to have any hope of securing their interests, protecting their sovereignty, and weathering the Great Disruption.

And to understand the EU's current thinking about its place in the world, Mark Leonard of the European Council on Foreign Relations put the question to Federica Mogherini, the High Representative of the European Union for Foreign Affairs and Security Policy. In a wide-ranging interview, Mogherini discusses the EU's efforts to boost its defense capacity, the future of UK-EU relations after Brexit, nuclear-arms control, migration, and many other issues.

Trump's Tariff Tantrum

In 2018, Trump began to implement his long-promised protectionist agenda, imposing tariffs on washing machines and solar panels, aluminum and steel, and a wide range of Chinese goods. But Pinelopi Koujianou Goldberg, the World Bank's new chief economist, reminds us that this is hardly the first time a US administration has resorted to tariffs to protect domestic jobs. More worrying, she thinks, are the Trump administration's attacks on the rules-based trade system. By creating so much international uncertainty, current US trade policies could have a chilling effect on investment, and thus on long-term growth.

For their part, Zhu Min, a former Deputy Managing Director of the International Monetary Fund who now teaches at Tsinghua University, and Miao Yanliang, Chief Economist of China's State Administration for Foreign Exchange, argue that the Trump administration's approach is self-defeating. Tariffs, they point out, will neither reduce the US's current-account deficit nor deter China from pursuing structural economic reforms in its effort to move up the global value chain. The Chinese economy, they conclude, "will continue to become more balanced and sustainable, regardless of the path the US chooses."

Similarly, Michael Froman, who served as US Trade Representative under President Barack Obama, notes that while Trump has been dumping boulders into America's harbors, many other countries have continued to deepen trade ties with one another. Still, Froman does not discount the threat of rising "nationalism, populism, nativism, and protectionism." If these forces are not met with measures

to ensure more economic inclusion and social mobility – particularly on the part of the business community – then they could augur "a significant historical rupture."

Finally, Dani Rodrik of Harvard University issues an important caveat: Just because the Trump administration's trade policies are misguided does not mean that the *status quo* is desirable or even sustainable. "The current system," Rodrik observes, "provides neither safeguards for maintaining high labor standards in advanced economies, nor adequate measures to prevent regulatory and tax arbitrage." As such, it is not a system that anyone should wish to preserve in its present form.

Regulating the Revolution

Another Gramscian observation about historical upheavals is that they often feature "passive revolutions" in which political and economic systems undergo profound change without society willing it. In the case of today's Silicon Valley "disruptors," passive revolution is the prevailing business model. Yet between Facebook's undue influence in political life and the "Uberization" of work, policymakers are only just beginning to grapple with the implications of digital platforms, let alone artificial intelligence and machine learning.

To Nobel laureate economist Jean Tirole, one thing is already clear: "A small cohort of technology firms now guards the door to the modern economy." Tirole thinks it is past time that policymakers and regulators acknowledged the inadequacy of current antitrust laws to account for the growing centrality of two-sided markets, network effects, and digital economies of scale. Looking ahead, he calls for a full rethinking of labor, privacy, and tax laws, lest digitalization come to represent an existential threat rather than an opportunity.

Agustín Carstens, General Manager of the Bank of International Settlements and a former Governor of the Bank of Mexico, thinks that fintech innovation, in particular, could present a significant opportunity for ensuring financial inclusion and boosting productivity. Still, he warns that without smart, proactive regulations and cross-border coordination, new technologies in this sector could "upset business models

that serve the greater good," increase financial-market volatility, exacerbate inequality, and introduce new consumer-protection concerns.

Taking a broader view, Raghuram G. Rajan, a former Governor of the Reserve Bank of India and a professor at the Chicago Booth School of Business, raises a number of concerns about the "growing dominance of leading technology firms" and the threats they pose to competition, efficiency, and innovation. He marshals ample evidence that fewer new firms are entering the market than in the past, cross-sector technological diffusion is slowing, rent-seeking is on the rise, and labor markets are no longer functioning in the interest of workers. Worse still, monetary policymakers are struggling to retain their independence at a time of declining trust in public institutions. Whether they can "navigate today's environment of distrust and derision" while still maintaining macroeconomic stability, Rajan concludes, "will be a key question in 2019 – and beyond."

Some governments are fueling that environment of distrust by manipulating official statistics. Nobel laureate economist Angus Deaton shows that the Trump administration has been finding more

and more ways to paper over domestic poverty, inequality, and other problems. In July 2018, Trump's Council of Economic Advisers went so far as to declare the War on Poverty "largely over." In reality, Deaton calculates that, "There are more 'globally poor' people in the US than in Sierra Leone or Nepal." And he laments that, whether it is poverty or the "unconscionable death toll following Hurricane Maria in Puerto Rico," the Trump administration will continue its war on truth in the coming year.

Meeting the Challenge

Unlike 2017, when the global economy sustained a synchronized expansion, 2018 was a year of emerging-market and stock-market jitters. With tightening monetary conditions in the US, an ongoing trade war, and other factors, Indonesian Minister of Finance Sri Mulyani Indrawati believes that the global economy – particularly emerging markets – are entering a "new age of volatility." Accordingly, she urges governments to come together "to speak with a single voice," as they did as recently as three years ago, when the Sustainable Development Goals were adopted. The alternative, she warns, is a zero-sum race to the bottom.

Célestin Monga, the Vice President and Chief Economist of the African Development Bank Group, agrees that developing- and emerging-economy governments must speak up for multilateralism. But he also calls on them to rethink their economic-development models, as many African countries have already begun to do. Rwanda, for example, made a bold decision in 2018 to risk a backlash from the US in order to defend its domestic garment industry with higher tariffs on imported secondhand clothing and footwear. In so doing, it is both reclaiming its dignity and adjusting to the realities of the twenty-first-century economy, where "global value chains are now the dominant framework for trade."

Finally, Klaus Schwab, Founder and Executive Chairman of the World Economic Forum, offers a preliminary blueprint describing how public- and private-sector leaders alike can manage an age of far-reaching change. What is needed, he contends, is "fresh thinking about what free, fair, and inclusive economic relations would actually look like in today's world." Yes, the international community must come together to redesign global-governance institutions, as it did after WWII. But it cannot stop there. "We are experiencing a fundamental change in how individuals and societies relate to each other," Schwab writes.

The goal for the year ahead, then, should be clear: to minimize the "morbid phenomena" that the Great Disruption has unleashed, and take steps to ensure that what emerges serves the public good. It is a goal shared by all of the contributors gathered here. **PS**

Roman Frydman
Kenneth Murphy
Jonathan Stein
Stuart Whatley

1:
CARDBOARD CUTOUTS OF FACEBOOK CEO MARK ZUCKERBERG STAND OUTSIDE THE US CAPITOL.

2:
ANTI-BREXIT DEMONSTRATORS IN LONDON.

A VERY TRUMPIAN

JOSEPH E. STIGLITZ
Nobel Laureate Economist

At the end of 2017, US President Donald Trump's administration and congressional Republicans rammed through a $1 trillion cut in corporate taxes, partly offset by tax increases for the majority of Americans in the middle of the income distribution. But in 2018, the US business community's jubilation over this handout started giving way to anxiety over Trump and his policies. ➔

YEAR

A year ago, US business and financial leaders' unbridled greed allowed them to look past their aversion to large deficits. But they are now seeing that the 2017 tax package was the most regressive and poorly timed tax bill in history. In the most unequal of all advanced economies, millions of struggling American families and future generations are paying for tax cuts for billionaires. The United States has the lowest life expectancy among all advanced economies, and yet the tax bill was designed so that 13 million more of its people will go without health insurance.

As a result of the legislation, the US Department of the Treasury is now forecasting a $1 trillion deficit for 2018 – the largest single-year non-recessionary peacetime deficit in any country *ever*. And if that were not bad enough, the promised increase in investment has not materialized. After giving a few pittances to workers, corporations have funneled most of the money into stock buybacks and dividends. But this isn't particularly surprising. Whereas investment benefits from certainty, Trump thrives on chaos.

Moreover, because the tax bill was rushed through, it is filled with mistakes, inconsistencies, and special-interest loopholes that were smuggled in when no one was looking. The legislation's lack of broad popular support all but ensures that much of it will be reversed when the political winds change, and this has not been lost on business owners.

As many of us noted at the time, the tax bill, along with a temporary increase in military spending, was not designed to give a sustained boost to the economy, but rather to provide the equivalent of a short-lived sugar high. Accelerated capital depreciation allows for higher after-tax profits now, but lower after-tax profits later. And because the legislation actually cut back on the deductibility of interest payments, it will ultimately increase the after-tax cost of capital, thus discouraging investment, much of which is financed by debt.

Meanwhile, the US's massive deficit will have to be financed somehow. Given the country's low saving rate, most of the money will inevitably come from foreign

> **Trump came to power by exploiting the broken promises of globalization, financialization, and trickle-down economics.**

1:
PRESIDENT TRUMP HOSTS KANYE WEST AT THE WHITE HOUSE.

2:
MOURNERS AT A CANDLELIGHT VIGIL FOR THE VICTIMS OF THE TREE OF LIFE SYNAGOGUE SHOOTING.

lenders, which means that the US will be sending large payments abroad to service its debt. A decade from now, total US income will most likely be lower than it would have been without the tax bill.

In addition to the disastrous tax legislation, the Trump administration's trade policies are also unsettling markets and disrupting supply chains. Many US export businesses that rely on Chinese inputs now have a good reason to move their operations out of the US. It is too soon to tally the costs of Trump's trade war, but it is safe to assume that everyone will be poorer as a result.

Likewise, Trump's anti-immigrant policies are encouraging companies that depend on engineers and other high-skilled workers to move their research labs and production facilities abroad. It is only a matter of time before we start seeing worker shortages elsewhere in the US.

Trump came to power by exploiting the broken promises of globalization, financialization, and trickle-down economics. After a global financial crisis and a decade of tepid growth, elites were discredited, and Trump emerged to assign blame. But, of course, neither immigration nor foreign imports has caused most of the economic problems that he has exploited for political gain. The loss of industrial jobs, for example, is largely due to technological change. In a sense, we have been the victims of our own success.

Still, policymakers certainly could have managed these changes better to ensure that the growth of national income accrued to the many, rather than the few. Business leaders and financiers have been blinded by their own greed, and the Republican Party, in particular, has been happy to give them whatever they want. As a result, real (inflation-adjusted) wages have stagnated, and those displaced by automation and globalization have been abandoned.

As if the economics of Trump's policies weren't bad enough, his politics are even worse. And, sadly, Trump's brand of racism, misogyny, and nationalist incitement has established franchises in Brazil, Hungary, Italy, Turkey, and elsewhere. All of these countries will experience similar – or worse – economic problems, just as all are facing the real-world consequences of the incivility on which their populist leaders thrive. In the US, Trump's rhetoric and actions have

2.

unleashed dark and violent forces that have already begun to spin out of control.

Society can function only when citizens have trust in their government, institutions, and one another. And yet, Trump's political formula is based on eroding trust and maximizing discord. One can only wonder where this will end. Is the murder of 11 Jews in a Pittsburgh synagogue the harbinger of an American *Kristallnacht*?

There is no way to know the answer to such questions. Much will depend on how the current political moment unfolds. If the supporters of today's populist leaders grow disillusioned with the inevitable failure of their economic policies, they could veer even further toward the neo-fascist right. More optimistically, they could be brought back into the liberal-democratic fold, or at least become demobilized by their disappointment.

This much we do know: economic and political outcomes are intertwined and mutually reinforcing. In 2019, the consequences of the bad policies and worse politics of the last two years will come more fully into view. PS

Joseph E. Stiglitz *is the winner of the 2001 Nobel Memorial Prize in Economic Sciences. His most recent book is* Globalization and its Discontents Revisited: Anti-Globalization in the Era of Trump.

MICHAEL BURLEIGH
Author and historian

T

hroughout 2018, analogies between today and the 1930s became alarmingly commonplace. Hortatory books such as former US Secretary of State Madeleine Albright's *Fascism: A Warning* and Yale University historian Timothy Snyder's *On Tyranny* are proliferating, and there certainly does seem to be a menacing odor of racism, violence, and despotic intrigue in the air.

In the United States, anti-Semites now march openly in the streets, and pipe bombs have targeted former President Barack Obama, Bill and Hillary Clinton, and the financier George Soros, and eight other prominent people singled out for attack by President Donald Trump. In Germany, leaders of the *Alternative für Deutschland* (AfD) think that Germans should be "proud" of the Wehrmacht's service in both world wars. In the United Kingdom, the right-wing thug Stephen Yaxley-Lennon has been canonized as an "English" martyr, and a supposedly reputable Sunday newspaper recently published talk of Tory Brexiteers "knifing" British Prime Minister Theresa May in the "killing zone." The list goes on.

Moreover, insurgent populists are not just marching. They are organizing a pan-European movement in the run-up to the May 2019 EU parliamentary elections. Rivals to lead this effort include Hungarian Prime Minister Viktor Orbán and Italian Deputy Prime Minister Matteo Salvini. Its would-be coordinator, though, is Steve Bannon, the burly American agitator who, together with the obscure Belgian politician Mischaël Modrikamen, has formed "The Movement."

Still, Bannon has had a mixed reception in nationalist and neo-fascist circles. As an American, he "has no place in a European political party," complained Jérôme Rivière of France's National Rally (formerly the National Front). Others, such as the Flemish nationalists in Vlaams Belang, suspect that Bannon is merely trying to create jobs for his friends, not least the Brexiteer Nigel Farage. ➔

History does not augur well for Bannon's efforts to divide and rule Europe on behalf of Trump and Russian President Vladimir Putin. The *Comitati d'Azione per l'Universalità di Roma* (CAUR), founded in 1933 to coordinate Europe's fascist movements, collapsed just two years later. The CAUR ended up being boycotted both by the Nazis and by the Italian Fascists who created it.

Once Hitler had overtaken Mussolini as the world's premier fascist, he no longer had an interest in anything other than acquiring clients and satraps. Moreover, he preferred to deal with "respectable" old elites such as Admiral Miklós Horthy of Hungary or Marshal Philippe Pétain of Vichy France.

In Europe today, the nationalist resurgence owes something to the proliferation of hysterical and inaccurate rhetoric comparing the EU to twentieth-century totalitarian regimes (a particular favorite of certain newspaper columnists who have blundered into politics). And, of course, the term "globalism" has become a serviceably sly synonym for Jews, just as "cosmopolitanism" was in the past.

But let's not get hung up on the "F" word. Today's Europe has not just emerged from a devastating world war that destroyed four empires; and today's politics are not dominated by paramilitary armies of demobilized veterans and students. The biggest danger that we face is not a straightforward revival of fascism, but rather a creeping shift in traditional conservatism toward the extreme nationalist/populist right.

From a historical perspective, then, we would do better to focus less on the threat of fascism, and more on the degeneration of conservatism before and after World War I. That is when the traditional conservative right became infected by authoritarian and corporatist ideas, as well as a hatred of the left, Jews, and teeming cosmopolitan metropolises such as Berlin, Madrid, and Vienna. At the time, those cities were red spots of modernism in a green sea of agrarian provincialism.

A decade before WWI, the Dreyfus Affair had already offered a striking preview of the deep-seated hatreds that would be mobilized 30 years later. By the time fascism had arrived, so too had Bolshevism. And that was enough for the traditional conservatives to hold their noses and throw in with the fascists, even if they were sniffy about the latter's shrill plebian tone. To understand what such an alliance might look like today, consider that Lord Pearson of the UK Independence Party recently hosted Yaxley-Lennon for lunch in the House of Lords.

This is not to say that conservativism and fascism are interchangeable concepts. In 1934, the Portuguese dictator António Salazar alluded to some important distinctions when he banned the National Syndicalist organization. Specifically, he objected to the group's "exaltation of youth, the cult of force through so-called direct action, the principle of the superiority of the state political power in social life, the propensity for organizing masses behind a single leader." Classical conservatives, after all, tend to favor demobilization and deference to authority and tradition, not mass-movement agitation in the streets.

Were he alive today, the great conservative thinker Eric Voegelin would cast a baleful eye over the conservatives who are now embracing "mobocracy," just as he did in the case of interwar German elites. And he would have been particularly scornful of the AfD's Beatrix von Storch, the Tory Brexiteer Jacob Rees-Mogg, and other members of the upper class who claim to be tribunes of the ordinary folk in "flyover" country.

> 66
>
> **Furthermore, one gathers that the educated middle classes are growing tired of being hectored by the self-appointed upper-class spokespeople of provincial ignorance.**
>
> 99

Likewise, Voegelin's acidic contemporary Karl Kraus would have had much to say about the debasement of language by right-wing newspapers that now smear civil servants and judges as "saboteurs" and "enemies of the people." And he would have skewered millionaire newspaper columnists who imagine that they know the mind of Everyman just because they call taxi drivers "mate."

Liberal democracy is not experiencing an existential crisis. Though the political pendulum has been swinging toward "identity," it will soon swing back toward "the economy" as we start to feel the full impact of the Fourth Industrial Revolution. Fundamental questions about the future of work and wages will reassert themselves with a vengeance.

Furthermore, one gathers that the educated middle classes are growing tired of being hectored by the self-appointed upper-class spokespeople of provincial ignorance. This would certainly explain the massive pro-EU demonstrations in London this past October, as well as the recent electoral successes of the Greens in Germany.

It is time for liberals to stop twittering away about fascism and tyranny, and start exposing the con artists and hucksters who have captured our politics. The conversation we should be having would focus squarely on the decay of modern conservatism, the crisis of social democracy, and the dawning age of technological disruption. **PS**

Michael Burleigh *is a historian and author. His books include* Small Wars, Faraway Places: The Genesis of the Modern World, Blood and Rage: A Cultural History of Terrorism, The Third Reich: A New History, *and* The Best of Times, the Worst of Times: A History of Now.

The New

Old Populism

For the better part of a century, populism was widely regarded as a distinctly Latin American phenomenon, a recurring political plague on countries such as Argentina, Ecuador, and Venezuela. In the last few years, however, populism has gone global, upending the politics of countries as diverse as Hungary, Italy, the Philippines, and the United States. Jair Bolsonaro, Brazil's president-elect, is the latest example of a larger trend.

Populist politicians gain traction when workers and middle-class citizens feel wronged by their countries' elites. In their unhappiness, voters turn to strong, charismatic personalities whose rhetoric often focuses on the causes and consequences of inequality. Moreover, populist leaders are nationalistic, and their currency is confrontation. Hence, "the people" must be pitted against the political establishment, large corporations, banks, multinationals, immigrants, and other foreign institutions.

Once in power, populist governments tend to implement policies aimed at redistributing income. More often than not, this entails unsustainable fiscal deficits and monetary expansion. Populist policies – which also include protectionism, discriminatory regulation, and capital controls – violate most of the core principles of traditional economics. But heterodoxy implies a break from the *status quo*. And according to populists, because the *status quo* is the source of their countries' ills, breaking with it is the only solution.

Venezuela offers a textbook example of how populism can take hold. The initial event that lent momentum to the country's populist movement occurred almost ten years before Hugo Chávez came to power. On February 27, 1989, riots erupted in the capital, Caracas, following an announcement that public transportation fares would rise by 30%. To reestablish order, the government was forced to call in the military. After five days of violence, more than 300 people had been killed.

This episode set the stage for Chávez's failed coup in February 1992. During the two years he spent in prison, Chávez prepared to run for the presidency, and when he was released, he visited town after town to present his populist program. The economy was struggling, and the poor adored him. In the December 1998 presidential election, he won by a landslide.

Similar deep-seated crises are behind the surge of right-wing populism today. In Brazil, Bolsonaro owes his sudden popularity to an economic and social crisis that has been brewing for almost a decade, producing high unemployment and undercutting wages across the board.

In Brazil, Bolsonaro owes his sudden popularity to an economic and social crisis that has been brewing for almost a decade.

Ultimately, lower- and middle-income households typically find themselves worse off than they were when the populist experiment was launched.

At the same time, the country has been mired in massive and successive corruption scandals that resulted in the jailing of former President Luiz Inácio Lula da Silva, and the impeachment and removal from office of his successor, Dilma Rousseff.

Likewise, the 2008 financial crisis laid the foundation for populism to emerge in developed countries. Ordinary citizens abhorred the bailout of the banks, and immigration crises in Europe and elsewhere added fuel to the nationalist fire.

There are many similarities between Latin America's experience with populism and that of the advanced economies today. Fiscal deficits in the US and some European countries are reaching new heights, and borrowing has risen to dangerous levels. The lesson from history is that a debt crisis could be in the offing.

There are also remarkable similarities with respect to how populist leaders actually conduct politics, particularly their emphasis on mobilizing public demonstrations of popular support. To be sure, US President Donald Trump's "MAGA" rallies are not the same as Chávez's mass marches. But Trump's mocking attacks against political adversaries, anti-globalization rhetoric, and contempt for elites are all familiar tropes to many Latin Americans. And like past Latin American populists, the Trump administration is pursuing a protectionist agenda to shield domestic industries from competition.

Moreover, Latin American populists have long made a point of condemning established institutions, particularly those that are supposed to provide checks and balances on the exercise of government power. Chávez criticized the Supreme Tribunal of Justice, and then packed it with loyalists; former Ecuadorian President Rafael Correa threatened to reform the country's stable monetary regime; and former Peruvian President Alan García launched scathing attacks against the International Monetary Fund.

Similarly, Trump has disparaged the US Federal Reserve as "crazy" and "*loco*" for its pursuit of monetary-policy normalization. And in Italy, where the government has proposed a budget that violates the European Union's deficit rules, Deputy Prime Minister Matteo Salvini has had harsh words for the European Central Bank and the European Commission.

Of course, there are also differences. Most important, many of the advanced economies where populist forces have made headway still have restrictions on monetary policy. Unlike in Latin America, the Fed and the ECB cannot be forced to finance governments' fiscal expenditures. Though Italy belongs to the eurozone, it has very little influence on how the ECB operates. So long as this remains the case, Italy's populist moment is unlikely to end with a major inflationary flare-up, as has traditionally been the case in Latin America. Argentina, for example, had 41% inflation immediately following the back-to-back presidencies of Néstor Kirchner and his wife, Cristina Fernández de Kirchner.

That said, there has been talk of a possible "Italeave," whereby Italy would exit the eurozone and reintroduce the lira. But Italians should understand that when other countries (for example, Liberia) have reintroduced a domestic currency, it has not ended well. Indeed, the most important lesson to take from Latin America's populist experiences is that they have invariably ended badly. Ultimately, lower- and middle-income households typically find themselves worse off than they were when the populist experiment was launched. **PS**

Sebastián Edwards *is Professor of International Business Economics at UCLA's Anderson Graduate School of Management. His latest book is* American Default: The Untold Story of FDR, the Supreme Court and the Battle Over Gold.

1:
SUPPORTERS OF
HUGO CHÁVEZ.

2:
JAIR BOLSONARO.

The Metamor of Centra Europe

IVAN KRASTEV
*Chairman of the Center
for Liberal Strategies*

phosis

I n Franz Kafka's novella *The Metamorphosis,* the protagonist Gregor Samsa awakens one morning "from uneasy dreams" to find that he has "transformed in his bed into a gigantic insect." Needless to say, Samsa's family is shocked and has no idea what to do with the ugly creature he has become.

Europeans know the feeling. In 2018, they were forced to acknowledge that Hungary and Poland have changed from promising models of liberal democracy into illiberal, conspiracy-minded majoritarian regimes. Now, the rest of Europe must decide what to do about the unfamiliar creatures residing in their house.

But first, it is worth considering why these illiberal transformations happened. Why have people who still see themselves as wholly European endorsed a revolt against the European Union, while embracing xenophobia and nativism? And why did liberals across Europe fail to respond in time?

Part of the problem is that liberal elites became complacent and overly confident in the power of EU institutions to contain populist upstarts. But, more than that, they failed to recognize that populism's appeal is more psychological than ideological.

To understand Central Europe's metamorphosis, bear in mind that the region's political imperative for almost three decades was "Imitate the West!" That process went by different names – democratization, liberalization, convergence, integration, Europeanization – but it was essentially an effort by post-communist reformers to import liberal-democratic institutions, adopt Western political and economic frameworks, and publicly embrace Western values. In practice, this meant that post-communist countries were compelled to adopt 20,000 new laws and regulations – none of which were really debated in their parliaments – to meet the requirements for accession to the EU.

In the event, adopting a foreign model of political economy turned out to have unexpected moral and psychological downsides. For the imitator, life becomes dominated by feelings of inadequacy, inferiority, dependency, and lost identity. Creating and inhabiting a credible copy of an idealized model requires never-ending criticism of – if not contempt for – one's identity up to that point. When an entire country undergoes this self-renunciation, a debilitating feeling of constantly being judged inevitably becomes endemic. After all, the realization of an ideal is, by definition, impossible. ➡

Across the region, the combination of an aging population, low birth rates, and mass emigration has stoked a demographic panic.

27%

IN THE PERIOD 1989–2017, LATVIA LOST 27% OF ITS POPULATION.

23%

LITHUANIA LOST 23% OF ITS POPULATION.

21%

BULGARIA LOST 21% OF ITS POPULATION.

3.4m

ROMANIA LOST 3.4 MILLION MEMBERS OF ITS POPULATION.

Not surprisingly, then, the post-1989 settlement created a festering sense of resentment. And today, that national *ressentiment* has become the driving force behind the nativist wave sweeping across Central and Eastern Europe. At the heart of the populist counter-revolution is a radical rejection of the imperative to imitate the liberal-democratic West.

Another contributing factor is the mass emigration from Central European countries following their accession to the EU. Depopulation helps to explain why countries that have benefited so much from the political and economic changes of the last two decades nevertheless feel a sense of loss, even trauma. Between 1989 and 2017, for example, Latvia, Lithuania, and Bulgaria hemorrhaged 27%, 23%, and 21% of their populations, respectively. Similarly, 3.4 million Romanians – the vast majority of them younger than 40 – have left their country since 2007. Across the region, the combination of an aging population, low birth rates, and mass emigration has stoked a demographic panic, which has paradoxically been expressed as a fear of African and Middle Eastern refugees (hardly any of whom have actually ended up in Central Europe).

Some Western Europeans have always complained about the free movement of people within the EU; but now many Central Europeans do, too, albeit for the opposite reason. Consider the example of a Bulgarian doctor who leaves his country in search of better professional opportunities in the Western part of the continent. He is not only depriving his country of his talents and skills, but also robbing it of the investment that it made by providing him with an education and other forms of social capital. The remittances that the doctor sends back

to his aging parents will not compensate for this loss.

This brings us back to the psychological dimension of Central Europe's metamorphosis. If you live in a country where the majority of young people cannot wait to leave, you will feel like a loser, regardless of how well you are doing. This unavoidable sense of loss and inferiority explains why Poland has become the poster child of the new populism. The fact that the same country has also registered declining levels of inequality, rising standards of living, and the fastest growth in Europe between 2007 and 2017 hardly matters.

As the principal advocates of the imitation imperative, post-communist liberals have come to be regarded as the political representatives of those who have left their countries, never to return. Meanwhile, the Western system that was supposed to serve as a model for Central Europe has descended into a crisis of its own.

It is little wonder, then, that those left behind in Central European societies have rejected imitation and raised the alarm over depopulation – even "ethnic disappearance." "The small nation," the novelist Milan Kundera once observed, "is one whose very existence may be put in question at any moment; a small nation can disappear and it knows it." Central Europeans already saw a world in which their cultures were vanishing. And with the rush of technological change and the threat of mass job displacement, they have come to perceive ethnic and cultural diversity as existential threats.

Still, while Central Europeans have lost their appetite for imitation, they also know that the disintegration of the

1:
PROTESTORS DEMONSTRATE
AS POLISH SENATORS VOTE TO
CHANGE THE JUDICIAL SYSTEM.

2:
HUNGARIAN PRIME MINISTER
VIKTOR ORBÁN.

EU would be an epic tragedy for their countries. A deepening of the East-West divide would not reverse depopulation, but it would threaten Central Europe's economic prospects. As a result, the region finds itself torn between reluctance to play the role of a pretender and fear that its own populist turn could precipitate a collapse of the EU. Either way, Central Europe's "uneasy dreams" have become a permanent reality. PS

Ivan Krastev is Chairman of the Center for Liberal Strategies in Sofia and the 2018–2019 Henry A. Kissinger Chair in Foreign Policy and International Relations at the John W. Kluge Center at the Library of Congress.

How Democracy Is Won

ANWAR IBRAHIM
Malaysian Political Leader

1.

It is perhaps indicative of our times that the peaceful transition of power by means of a democratic election is a candidate for "Disruption of the Year." The outcome of the Malaysian general election in May was the hopeful outlier to a global trend toward populist nationalism, engineered through fear of refugees, migrants, and the "other."

Malaysia is a Muslim-majority country where democratic values and collaboration between all groups made change possible. The electoral disruption was hardly what the world expected or what the pundits predicted, so we would do well to take careful note of what Malaysia's voters cast their ballots to achieve.

For starters, Malaysians voted to end the rule of a coalition, the Barisan Nasional (BN), dominated by the United Malays National Organization (UMNO), which had been in power since the country gained its independence from Britain in 1957. With the demise of BN came an end to the hegemony of communal race-based politics. Moreover, voters rejected a system of governance that was operating as a conduit for transferring public goods and opportunities to private individuals and groups.

Under the previous system, the government had become an omnipresent factor in business and all aspects of social development. In return for what it gave through transfers, it expected unflinching electoral support, regardless of the circumstances or the competence of its candidates. Electoral feudalism was essentially the Malaysian way for the long decades of UNMO rule: voters were tied to their political masters.

The great disruption of May 2018 was driven by popular revulsion at the flagrant corruption that had become endemic in Malaysian governance. The figures are staggering. Untold billions have disappeared from the public purse through the scandal at the 1Malaysia Development Berhad (1MDB) fund and nefarious spending practices across government ministries.

1:
ANWAR IBRAHIM ADDRESSES A RALLY.

2:
STUDENTS WAVE FLAGS AT MERDEKA
SQUARE IN KUALA LUMPUR.

2.

The arrogance and openness of corruption trickled down more effectively and extensively than the effects of any development program. When the rich lavishly reward themselves, it is little wonder that those further down the pecking order – whose living standards are steadily declining – are tempted to follow suit. The sense that the whole of Malaysian society was being corroded convinced voters that only radical change would do.

The roots of change, however, extend much deeper than one electoral cycle. The groundwork for Malaysia's democratic disruption was laid during 20 years of campaigning for reform. It has been part of every election since 1998, when I was summarily dismissed from government and arrested on trumped-up charges.

The reform agenda, developed by Parti Keadilan Rakyat (PKR), gradually changed the political landscape. In the 2013 election, our opposition coalition actually won the popular vote but could not overturn the gerrymandered allocation of seats in Malaysia's first-past-the-post system.

The decline in national life eventually brought Malaysia's longest-serving prime minister, Tun Dr. Mahathir Mohamad, out of retirement at the age of 92. It is no secret that Tun Mahathir and I have had a stormy relationship in the past. So, when he came to visit me in prison to discuss joining our opposition coalition, it was clear that we had achieved critical mass.

Nothing would seem as disruptive (in the sense of unexpected) as two erstwhile political adversaries collaborating. It required genuine forgiveness and a radical change in personal perspective, so that politics could move forward for the sake

of the country. The Pakatan Harapan coalition won the election, and after 20 years of effort, PKR emerged as one of the largest single parties. According to our pre-election agreement, Tun Mahathir became our new prime minister.

The new coalition government has committed itself to a reform agenda that envisions Malaysia as a fully mature, just, equitable, and effective democracy. Ending corruption is but one item on our agenda. Establishing an independent judiciary, election commission, and free press, and nurturing active civil-society organizations, are also necessary to ensure free, fair, and open elections, deliver justice, and see that there is an equitable provision of public goods and services.

Another aspect of democratic maturity has been the move away from communalism toward genuine meritocracy, inclusive and just to all of Malaysia's citizens. Affirmative action was introduced to help the Malay and the Bumiputera communities overcome the deficiencies they inherited as a result of intentional colonial neglect. But, over time, and under the UNMO, positive discrimination became an entrenched system of handouts treated as entitlements, which stultified enterprise and ambition. Affirmative action became a prop for complacency and corruption, rather than a helping hand.

Malaysia will now help the poor by offering assistance to those in need, regardless of their communal origins. The needs of poor rural Malays will in no way be favored – or disfavored. Need qualifies the needy. Making distinctions based on race, ethnicity, and communal origins has nothing to do with fighting poverty.

Malaysia's strength is its plurality, yet we have much work to do to restore the openness and genuine engagement of our multicultural society. There is much to be gained from sharing the richness and creative potential of our varied traditions, languages, cultures, and ideas. Through reform and cooperation, Malaysia will become a more vibrant, productive society, and a model of peaceful, democratic coexistence that the world so desperately needs.

My perspective on the change that has unfolded so far is quite particular. At the start of 2018, I was still in prison, confined by the government's determination to prevent my participation in the elections. So, for me, 2018 has been momentous.

The coalition we negotiated – even with me still behind bars – swept to a resounding and unexpected victory. Within days, I was released from prison and received a royal pardon. Within months, I had stood for and won a by-election that returned me to parliament. And now, I am working to insure the implementation of the reform agenda and the fulfilment of decades of determination to effect real change.

If this is disruption, I look forward to more of it in 2019 and beyond. **PS**

Anwar Ibrahim, *a member of Malaysia's parliament, is President of the Parti Keadilan Rakyat and Leader of the Pakatan Harapan coalition.*

PS. Subscribe Now.

Access unrivaled insights about the issues shaping your world.

🗓 Annual Subscription

Includes access to:

- **PS On Point**, exclusive long-form commentaries, book reviews, and interviews with leading experts, delivered weekly

- **PS The Big Picture**, collections of curated commentaries on the topics driving the global conversation

- **The Year Ahead**, our annual print magazine, shipped to your door for free

- **PS Podcasts**, a hub for dialogues on the world's pressing issues

- **Videos and short films** featuring our contributors

- **PS digital archive**

- A complimentary *Project Syndicate* tote bag

$100 PER YEAR

 ### Bring *Project Syndicate* content to your company or classroom

Group subscriptions are available at advantageous rates for companies, organizations, or academic institutions.

Please contact us to discuss a subscription plan that's right for you.

Contact us at subscriptions@project–syndicate.org for more details.

project–syndicate.org/subscribe

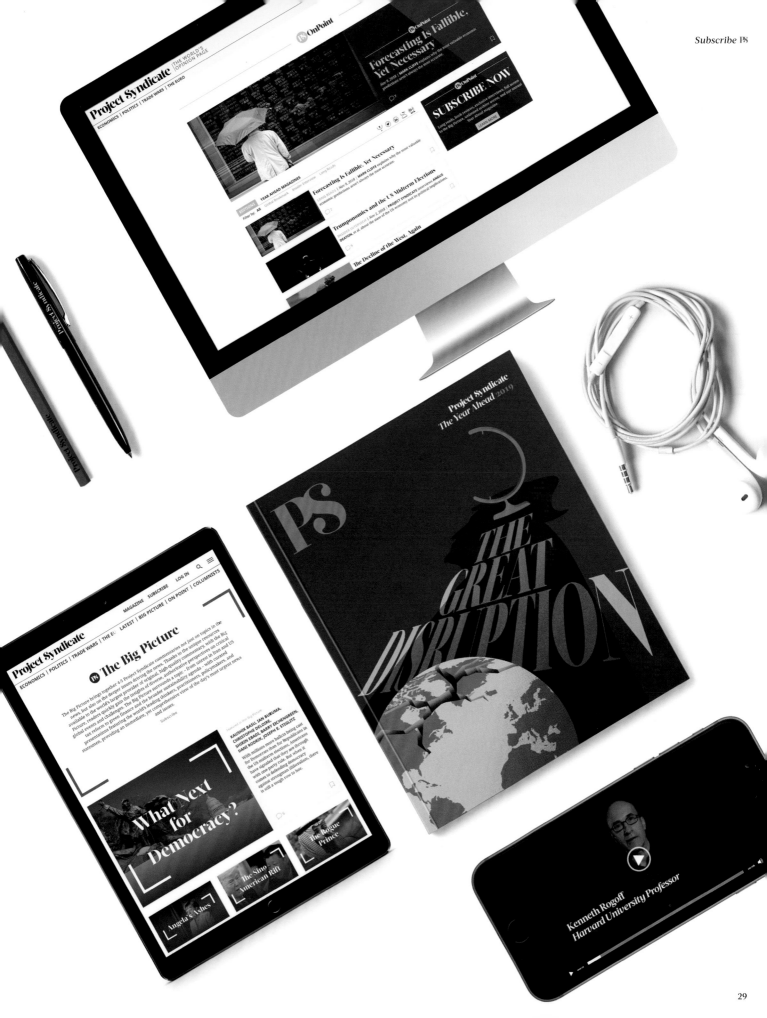

Globalization at a Crossroads

GORDON BROWN
Former British Prime Minister

Whether or not one realizes it, 2018 may have been a historic turning point. Poorly managed globalization has led to nationalist "take-back-control" movements and a rising wave of protectionism that is undermining the 70-year-old American-led international order. The stage is set for China to develop its own parallel international institutions, auguring a world divided between two competing global-governance systems.

1.

Whatever happens in the next few years, it is already clear that the 2008-2018 decade marked an epochal shift in the balance of economic power. When I chaired the Group of Twenty (G20) London Summit at the height of the global financial crisis, North America and Europe comprised around 15% of the world's population, but accounted for 57% of total economic activity, 61% of investment, around 50% of manufacturing, and 61% of global consumer spending.

But the world's economic center of gravity has shifted since then. Whereas around 40% of production, manufacturing, trade, and investment was located outside the West in 2008, over 60% is today. Some analysts predict that Asia will account for 50% of global economic output by 2050. True, China's *per capita* income might still be less than half that of the United States in 2050; but the sheer size of the Chinese economy will nonetheless raise new questions about global governance and geopolitics.

Under New Management

For decades after its formation in the 1970s, the Group of Seven (G7) – Canada, France, Germany, Italy, Japan, the United Kingdom, and the US – essentially presided over the entire world economy. But by 2008, I and others had begun to discern a changing of the guard. Behind the scenes, North American and European leaders were debating whether it was time to create a new premier forum for economic cooperation that would include emerging economies.

These debates were often heated. On one side were those who wanted to keep the group small (one early US proposal envisioned a G7+5); on the other side were those who wanted the group to be as inclusive as possible. To this day, the results of those earlier negotiations are not fully understood. When the G20 met in London in April 2009, it actually included 23 countries – with Ethiopia representing Africa, Thailand representing Southeast Asia, and the Netherlands and Spain joining the original European list – as well as the European Union. Nonetheless, even that *de facto* G24 did not fully reflect how fast the world was changing. Today, Nigeria, Thailand, Iran, and the United Arab Emirates' economies are each larger than the smallest G20 economy (South Africa), yet none of these countries is a member.

Likewise, the ground is also shifting beneath the International Monetary Fund. When the original IMF Articles of Agreement were being negotiated in 1944, there was some disagreement over whether the new body should be headquartered in Europe or the US. Eventually, it was decided that it should be based in the capital city of the country with the largest share of voting rights (which tracks a country's share of the global economy). This means that, within a decade or two, China could demand that the IMF be headquartered in Beijing.

To be sure, the IMF most likely will not relocate from Washington, DC (America would leave the IMF before the IMF leaves America). But the point remains: the world is experiencing an epochal rebalancing that is not just economic, but also geopolitical. Unless the West can find a way to uphold multilateralism in an increasingly multipolar world, China will continue to develop alternative financial and governance institutions, as it has with the establishment of the Asian Infrastructure Investment Bank (AIIB) and the Shanghai Cooperation Organization.

Hollow Sovereignty

The current trade conflict between the United States and China is symptomatic of a larger transition in global financial power. On the surface, the Trump administration's confrontation with China is about trade, with disputes over currency manipulation thrown in for good measure. But from Trump's speeches, one gathers that the real battle is about something bigger: the future of technological dominance and global economic power.

While Trump at least detects the growing threat to American supremacy, he has ignored the most obvious strategy for responding to it: namely, a united front with US allies and partners around the world. Instead, Trump has asserted a prerogative to act unilaterally, as if America still rules over a unipolar world. As a result, a trail of geopolitical ruin already lies in his wake.

Among other things, Trump has pulled out of the Iran nuclear deal and the Paris climate agreement, and announced that the US is withdrawing from the 31-year-old Intermediate-Range Nuclear Forces Treaty with Russia. Moreover, his administration has blocked the ➡

PREDICTED SHARE OF GLOBAL ECONOMIC OUTPUT FOR ASIA BY 2050.

50%

1:
GORDON BROWN.

1:
WORLD LEADERS GATHER
FOR THE G20 SUMMIT IN
HANGZHOU, CHINA.

2:
MULTINATIONAL COOPERATION
ABOARD THE INTERNATIONAL
SPACE STATION.

appointment of judges to the World Trade Organization's dispute-settlement body; reduced the G7 and G20 to near-irrelevance; and ditched the Trans-Pacific Partnership, opening the door for China to assert its economic dominance in the Asia-Pacific region.

There is a deep irony here. When America actually did preside over a unipolar world, it generally preferred to act through multilateral institutions. But now that the world is becoming more multipolar, the Trump administration is going it alone. The question is whether this effort to reclaim an undiluted form of nineteenth-century sovereignty could ever work.

With respect to trade, the Trump administration's "America First" policies might initially appear to reduce imports. But they are also affecting imported inputs for US exports, which will not be spared from the damaging effects of higher trade barriers. Making matters worse, the current wave of protectionism may be creating new fiscal pressures, as US manufacturing workers and struggling farmers demand compensation through subsidies or tax relief.

Storm Clouds Forming

For an even starker illustration of the dangers posed by protectionism and expansionary US fiscal policies, consider what would happen in the event of another global economic downturn. In 2008, governments around the world were able to cut interest rates, introduce unconventional monetary policies, and pursue fiscal stimulus. Moreover, these efforts were coordinated globally to maximize their effect. Central banks worked closely together, and with the G20 leaders' summit in 2009, there was unparalleled cooperation between global heads of state and finance ministries.

Now, look ahead to the 2020s, when there will be far less monetary and fiscal room for maneuver. Interest rates will almost certainly be too low for monetary policymakers to provide an effective stimulus; and the massive balance sheets inherited from the last crisis will have made central bankers wary of further quantitative easing.

Fiscal policy will be similarly constrained. As of 2018, the EU's average government debt-to-GDP ratio stands above 80%; the US federal deficit is on track to exceed 5% of GDP; and China is dealing with mounting public and private debt. Under these conditions, providing fiscal stimulus will be even more difficult than in the years following the last crisis, and cross-border coordination will be even more necessary. Sadly, current trends suggest that governments will be more likely to blame one another than to cooperate to put things right.

We are thus faced with a paradox. Discontent over globalization has brought a new wave of protectionism and unilateralism, but addressing the sources of that discontent can only be accomplished through cooperation. No one country can solve problems such as rising inequality, wage stagnation, financial instability, tax avoidance and evasion, climate change, and refugee and migration crises. A retreat to nineteenth-century great-power politics could decisively set back the prosperity that we have achieved in the twenty-first century.

Far from representing a clear strategic view of the future, though, "America First" is more like a spasm of self-harm by a once-hegemonic power still clinging to the past. To hark back to the nationalism expressed in the Treaty of Versailles is to ignore the indispensable difference that enhanced intergovernmental action can make.

The Case for Hope

As America turns away from multilateralism, China is reshaping global geopolitics on its own through the AIIB, the New Development Bank, the Belt and Road Initiative, and other means. But, though China's current policies will have long-term implications for the Asia-Pacific region and the world, most of us have yet to consider these consequences with appropriate care.

Still, great-power confrontations need not be the new order of the day. The failed launch in October of a rocket carrying a US astronaut and a Russian cosmonaut to the International Space Station was a fitting metaphor for the state of geopolitical relations today. Nonetheless, it also served as a reminder of a deeper history of multilateral cooperation and what it has accomplished. All told, 18 countries have participated in voyages to the ISS, which is currently home to a team of American, Russian, and German astronauts working together.

Though the space race began as a zero-sum contest at the height of the Cold War, it became an area of sustained international collaboration. Today, the Russian and US space programs are so mutually dependent that American astronauts cannot fly to the ISS without Russian rocket launchers, and Russian cosmonauts cannot survive aboard the station without American technology.

Of course, this longstanding partnership could well end. And a 2011 US law already bars China from accessing the ISS, or from working with the US National Aeronautics and Space Administration (NASA). Still, if otherwise hostile powers such as the US and Russia can find ways to cooperate in space, then surely something similar can be achieved here on Earth.

We must hold out hope. The Cold War lasted four agonizing decades, not least because the Soviet Union refused to acknowledge the value of markets and private property, and eschewed contact with the West. The same cannot be said for China. More than 600,000 Chinese students study abroad every year, and 450,000 of them do so in the US and Europe, where they form lasting social and professional networks.

As we prepare for global conflicts in the years ahead, we must work for a future shaped by collaboration. Whether the issue is financial stability, climate change, or tax havens, there is a strong case to be made that national interests are best served through international cooperation. Yet with supply chains being reorganized, bilateral and regional trade agreements being negotiated, and regional governments – not least that of California – pursuing their own deals at the global level, we will have to expand the scope of that cooperation.

Globalization is at a crossroads. One way or another, international organizations and multilateral frameworks will need to accommodate the new "poles" of geopolitical power that are emerging. The decisions that we are contemplating today will have significant and far-reaching implications for our planet's future. The only question is whether they will be made unilaterally or collaboratively. We must summon the will of our postwar predecessors, so that we, too, can be "present at the creation" of an order that is fit for our moment in history. **PS**

As we prepare for global conflicts in the years ahead, we must work for a future shaped by collaboration.

Gordon Brown, former Prime Minister and Chancellor of the Exchequer of the United Kingdom, is United Nations Special Envoy for Global Education and Chair of the International Commission on Financing Global Education Opportunity. He chairs the Advisory Board of the Catalyst Foundation.

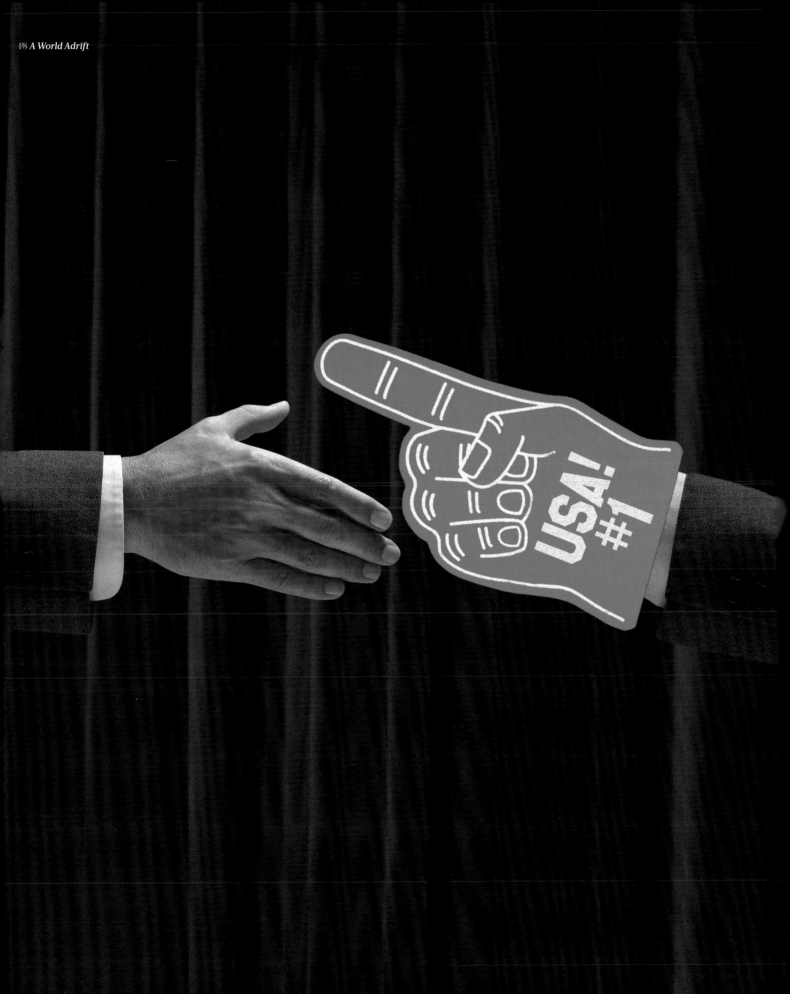

Transatlanticism, Interrupted

JULIANNE SMITH
*Deputy National Security Adviser
to former Vice President Joe Biden*

O f all the smears that US President Donald Trump has made, his mendacious claims about the European Union are perhaps the most egregious. "Nobody treats us much worse than the European Union," Trump said in October. "The European Union was formed in order to take advantage of us on trade, and that's what they've done."

> **" Consider the nearly two-year litany of abuse from the White House. "**

Obviously, nothing could be further from the truth. Yet whenever I raise concerns over comments like these with friends serving in the Trump administration, I always get the same response: ignore the rhetoric and the tweets; pay attention to the policies. Should those of us who worry about America's longstanding alliances be reassured by this argument?

On one hand, some of the Trump administration's policies – not least the significant increase in funding for the European Deterrence Initiative – do indeed reflect a firm commitment to America's European allies. But, on the other hand, such policies are not enough to counter the lasting damage that Trump is inflicting on the transatlantic relationship with his destructive rhetoric and evident contempt for Europe.

Consider the nearly two-year litany of abuse from the White House. Since his inauguration, Trump has accused London Mayor Sadiq Khan of "doing a very bad job on terrorism." He has falsely claimed that crime in Germany is up and alluded to a terrorist attack in Sweden that never happened. He has explicitly described the EU as a "foe." And he has also accused Federica Mogherini, EU High Representative for Foreign Affairs and Security Policy, of hating America. ➔

1:
JULIANNE SMITH.

1:
WORLD LEADERS MEET
IN BRUSSELS FOR THE
2018 NATO SUMMIT.

17%

NUMBER OF REPUBLICANS
WANTING TO WITHDRAW
THE US FROM NATO IN 2016.

38%

NUMBER OF REPUBLICANS
WANTING TO WITHDRAW
THE US FROM NATO IN 2018.

1.

On their own, such statements (there are many more) represent a stark departure from the language that previous US presidents have used to describe America's European friends. But Trump's words are even more disturbing when compared to the flattering language he uses to describe US adversaries.

Does it matter that Trump praises Russian President Vladimir Putin and North Korean dictator Kim Jong-un at the same time that he criticizes German Chancellor Angela Merkel? Recent polling suggests that it does. For the past 18 years, whether Americans looked at Russia with suspicion, disdain, or hope, Republicans and Democrats alike have viewed that country largely through the same lens. But Trump's inexplicable praise for Putin has chipped away at that bipartisan consensus. According to a July 2018 Gallup survey, Republicans are now almost twice as likely as Democrats to view Russia favorably.

Likewise, there is evidence that Trump's disparaging remarks about NATO are disrupting the bipartisan support that the alliance has enjoyed for over 70 years. Between 2016 and 2018, the percentage of Republicans who told YouGov that they wanted to withdraw from NATO jumped from 17% to 38%, with another 38% supporting continued membership. Suddenly, a party with a long tradition of backing military alliances is now deadlocked on the fundamental question of NATO.

Beyond politicizing issues that were once bipartisan, Trump is also actively undermining the European project. Since the EU's creation, US presidents of both parties have assumed correctly that "an ever closer union" is in America's national interest. Trump has brought that tradition to an abrupt end. Not only has he openly encouraged EU member states to quit the bloc; he has also slapped tariffs on EU exports to the US. And by abandoning the Iran nuclear deal, he has sabotaged one of the signature achievements of EU-US cooperation in recent years.

By weakening Western unity, leaving ambassadorial posts across Europe unfilled, and launching personal attacks against European leaders, Trump has made his intent clear. He is divesting America's holdings in the transatlantic relationship, and abandoning America's traditional leadership role both on the world stage and within institutions like NATO. Though Trump and his cabinet members still attend ministerial meetings

1:
A POLISH SOLDIER DURING
NATO MILITARY EXERCISES.

2:
NATO SECRETARY GENERAL
JENS STOLTENBERG.

2.

By weakening Western unity, leaving ambassadorial posts across Europe unfilled, and launching personal attacks against European leaders, Trump has made his intent clear.

and summits, their participation hardly rises to the level of leadership.

Consider the NATO summit in July 2018. Almost all of the policy "deliverables" had already been agreed to and finalized months earlier, and were merely repackaged to give NATO leaders something to celebrate. Even the reform of the alliance's military command structure – the crown jewel of this year's summit – had been finalized months earlier among defense ministers. There was at least some progress toward closing readiness and mobility gaps; but those achievements were drowned out by Trump's tantrum over defense spending, an important issue that is ill-served by added drama.

Instead of pushing NATO to grapple with tough issues such as artificial intelligence and space exploration/militarization, Trump's advisers have decided that simply getting their boss to show up is a deliverable in itself. But NATO can run on autopilot for only so long. Four or even eight years without an American hand at the controls could leave the alliance's resolve, unity, and capabilities irreversibly diminished.

America's ties with Europe have always been complicated and riddled with policy disputes. But, unlike past presidents, Trump questions the basic value of the transatlantic relationship. In seeking to undermine it, he has thrown in his lot with the likes of Putin, Hungarian Prime Minister Viktor Orbán, and Chinese President Xi Jinping.

When the 46th president of the United States takes office, he or she should not hold any illusions about what it will take to repair the damage Trump has done. Whether it is January 2021 or 2025, merely returning to the post-war *status quo* will not be an option. To reinvest in the transatlantic relationship, we will first have to redefine it. The coming year would not be too early to start thinking creatively about new paths for cooperation. **PS**

Julianne Smith, *deputy national security adviser to former Vice President Joe Biden, is currently a fellow at the Center for a New American Security and a visiting fellow at the Bosch Academy in Berlin.*

ZED

CHAOS

The Trumping of the Middle East

———

SHLOMO BEN-AMI
Former Israeli Foreign Minister

US President Donald Trump may be mercurial, but he does have a doctrine. As his speech in September at the United Nations General Assembly again confirmed, Trump rejects multilateral institutions and liberal values in favor of the nation-state and power politics. But understanding the "Trump doctrine" – with its support for abandoning America's longstanding role as a global arbiter – does not make it any less disruptive, especially for the already-unstable Middle East.

Under Trump, in a sinister reversal of America's Cold War victory, the Middle East has become Russia's playground.

It is no surprise that the Middle East has been particularly vulnerable to the unsettling effects of the Trump doctrine. After all, the timid policies of Trump's immediate predecessor, Barack Obama, significantly exacerbated the region's dysfunction, opening the way for Trump to introduce what can only be described as mayhem.

For starters, the Obama administration utterly failed to make progress in resolving the Israeli-Palestinian conflict – a failure Trump promised to correct with the "deal of the century." Instead, Trump has unilaterally recognized Jerusalem as the capital of Israel, moving the US embassy there, and ended financial support to the United Nations Relief and Works Agency (UNRWA), which supports more than five million registered Palestinian refugees. One must be extraordinarily ignorant to believe Trump's claims that these actions amount to taking two of the thorniest issues in the Israeli-Palestinian conflict "off the table."

Making matters worse, by abandoning efforts to overthrow Syrian dictator Bashar al-Assad, the Obama administration opened the door for Russia to move into the region. Under Trump, in a sinister reversal of America's Cold War victory, the Middle East has become Russia's playground.

Egypt, a close US ally, has signed huge arms deals with Russia, which is also providing four nuclear-power reactors to the country. The bilateral relationship has been deepened through close military cooperation in Libya – a country that, totally ignored by the United States, has become a vital strategic link in Russia's penetration of the Western sphere of influence, exemplified by the Kremlin's efforts to build a naval base there.

Saudi Arabia, which has long benefited from America's security umbrella, has also purchased nuclear-power reactors and advanced S-400 missiles from Russia. And Bahrain, Morocco, and the United Arab Emirates are pursuing arms deals with Russia.

Turkey, a key NATO ally, is also moving into Russia's strategic orbit. When it comes to his country's faltering economy and democratic backsliding, President Recep Tayyip Erdoğan has much to answer for. But the Trump administration's decision in August to double US tariffs on steel and aluminum as punishment for

Turkey's refusal to release an American cleric arrested for alleged "subversive activities" undoubtedly contributed to the lira's collapse. In fact, the Trump administration has offered no indication that it cares whether Turkey remains a US ally at all.

Even Israel, which Trump has done so much to appease, is drifting toward Russia, on which it depends to help it prevent Iran from gaining a foothold in Syria. With the Trump administration offering nothing resembling an effective Syria policy, much less a strategy for reining in Iran's drive to secure a land corridor to Lebanon, Israeli Prime Minister Binyamin Netanyahu now makes regular pilgrimages to Moscow to plead Israel's case.

The dangers raised by Trump's policies toward Iran cannot be overstated. Withdrawing the US from the Joint Comprehensive Plan of Action (JCPOA), the most important nuclear non-proliferation agreement in a quarter-century, and imposing a strict sanctions regime on Iran have failed to derail the latter's bellicose strategy for achieving regional primacy, exemplified by its activities in Lebanon, Syria, and Yemen. These policies have also undermined America's own global standing, including by widening the rift between the US and its European allies, all of which support the JCPOA.

Now, Syria is at risk of becoming the site of a major war between Israel, which is already conducting military drills, and the alliance of Iran and its Lebanese proxy, Hezbollah. Such a war, if it comes, could also engulf Lebanon. In all the turmoil, Israel could even end up clashing with Russia.

Consider the recent downing of a Russian military plane by Syrian anti-aircraft fire. Because the accident – which killed all 15 people aboard the plane – occurred amid an Israeli attack on Iranian installations, Russia's military, already fed up with the Israeli air force's supposed impudence, blamed Israeli jets for putting the Russian plane in the line of fire. Now, Russian President Vladimir Putin appears to be planning to send missiles to Syria to help counteract the Israeli air force's dominance of that country's air space.

But Syria is far from the only country that is in danger. Trump's policy of emboldening Iran's rivals – Egypt, Israel, and Saudi Arabia – could also trigger escalations in the conflicts in Bahrain, Lebanon, and Yemen, not to mention Gaza.

Instead of promoting a diplomatic settlement to end the colossal humanitarian tragedy in Yemen, Trump is providing Saudi Arabia's Crown Prince Mohammed bin Salman with all the weapons he needs to prosecute a war that his country seems incapable of winning. That is on top of Trump's abandonment of Obama's calls for democratic reform – a gift to both the House of Saud and Egypt's President Abdel Fattah el-Sisi.

Under Trump, the US has established itself as a deeply disruptive force not just in the Middle East, but throughout the world. Instead of resolving conflicts, Trump's administration exacerbates them, in the illusory belief that supporting autocrats and punishing adversaries with sanctions, tariffs, and the withdrawal of aid will facilitate negotiations later.

But, as the Arab Spring showed, there is a limit to the capacity of the Middle East's autocracies to stifle the ambitions and frustrations of its burgeoning young population. When that capacity is depleted and the region is plunged into chaos, the Trump doctrine will have nothing to offer, because, in a sense, it will have achieved its goal. **PS**

1.

2.

Shlomo Ben-Ami, *a former Israeli foreign minister, is Vice President of the Toledo International Center for Peace. He is the author of* Scars of War, Wounds of Peace: The Israeli-Arab Tragedy.

1:
AN IRANIAN ARMY CLERIC STANDS NEAR A S-200 SURFACE-TO-AIR MISSILE.

2:
THE ONGOING HUMANITARIAN CRISIS IN YEMEN.

Korea's Year of Living Diplomatically

YOON YOUNG-KWAN
*Former South Korean
Minister of Foreign Affairs*

South Korea probably endured more political turbulence than almost any other country in 2018. On the domestic front, the new liberal government of President Moon Jae-in forged ahead with measures to address entrenched corruption, and implemented progressive (and hotly debated) economic policies to help low-income people. But these important changes were dwarfed by the wave of disruption from abroad.

Few South Koreans had expected that US President Donald Trump would show such determination in undermining the post-war liberal international order. That order has served as a foundation for Korea's economic growth and democratic development since the 1960s. Now that it is under threat, South Koreans are anxiously wondering whether Trump will be a one-term outlier or an agent of permanent change.

After Trump's April 2017 threat to "terminate" the "horrible" free-trade agreement which for a decade has backstopped a strategic alliance with the United States that has lasted for more than half a century, South Koreans were relieved to see Trump and Moon sign a revised deal in September. Still, the Trump administration's trade war with China is certain to strike a severe economic blow to South Korea.

"It will be one of the hardest-hit economies in the world if an all-out trade war breaks out," a senior trade official warned – and this when the economy is already slowing. If Moon fails to address the challenges of a shrinking working-age population and rising inequality, South Korea could end up with a Trump of its own.

On a more positive note, fears of a military conflict on the Korean Peninsula have subsided. In November 2017, some US foreign-policy experts put the chances of a war with North Korea as high as 50%. Yet today, the US and South Korea are working with the North to find a viable formula for denuclearization and a lasting peace. In this regard, 2018 was a pivotal year. The transition from crisis to diplomacy began when North Korean leader Kim Jong-un responded favorably in a New Year's address to overtures from Moon; but it owes much of its momentum to Trump's bold political approach.

Moon had been signaling his openness for dialogue with North Korea since taking office in May 2017, even inviting North Korean athletes to participate in the Pyeongchang Winter Olympics in February 2018. This set the stage for inter-Korean dialogue. During a visit by a South Korean special envoy to Pyongyang, Kim indicated for the first time that he might give up his nuclear program, and that he wanted to meet with Trump to discuss it. Since then, Kim has said that he will depart from the "byungjin line" – the parallel development of nuclear weapons and the North Korean economy – to focus solely on economic development.

After three rounds of inter-Korean summit meetings, Moon and Kim signed the Pyongyang Joint Declaration on September 19. Both sides committed to turning the Korean Peninsula into "a land of peace free from nuclear weapons and nuclear threats"; and North Korea promised that it will dismantle its Dongchang-ri missile engine test site and launch platform. Both sides have also agreed "to expand the cessation of military hostilities in regions of confrontation," including the demilitarized zone on the border and the Northern Limit Line in the West Sea. All told, the joint declaration represents meaningful progress toward lowering the probability of a conventional military confrontation, which is actually more likely than a nuclear war.

Meanwhile, at the historic Trump-Kim summit in Singapore on June 12, the US and North Korea reached a four-point agreement expressing "the desire of the peoples of the two countries for peace and prosperity." But while this joint ➡

> ## 66
> ## Yes, one cannot be too careful when dealing with the Kim regime; but nor should one be surprised that a young leader might pursue a different strategy from his father's.
> ## 99

statement marked an important shift in US diplomacy, it was criticized for lacking details about the timeline and method of denuclearization. To address these issues, US Secretary of State Mike Pompeo has continued to meet with the North Koreans, visiting Pyongyang four times over the course of the year.

After returning from his last visit, when he met with Kim for three and a half hours, Pompeo reported that unspecified progress had been made toward denuclearizing the North. But many specialists and observers are skeptical. The Kim regime, after all, has yet to take any serious action despite the flurry of talks.

What happens next is anyone's guess. But even skeptics in the US would agree that continued diplomacy is preferable to the saber rattling of 2017. Looking ahead, much will depend on US policymakers' willingness to be pragmatic in dealing with the Kim regime. Addressing the threat of a nuclear-armed North Korea is as much a matter of perception as deterrence. A small, isolated, and economically devastated country that is surrounded by major powers will feel insecure under any circumstances.

As such, Kim will not give up his nuclear weapons until he is sure that his regime can prosper without them. But while many US policymakers already know that addressing the regime's security concerns is a prerequisite for denuclearization, there has not been any real action on this front. Moreover, it remains to be seen if the Trump administration can mobilize the necessary support from Congress to move the process along.

For example, the US might consider a declaration of peace to end the Korean War. Barring that, it could establish a liaison office in Pyongyang, or extend humanitarian aid to the North (outside of economic sanctions). Or, it could invite North Korean sports teams, performers, bureaucrats, and students to participate in cultural events or pursue educational opportunities in the West, thus exposing them to liberal democracy and a market economy. None of these options weakens sanctions, which can remain in place until the Kim regime follows through on denuclearization.

Kim has already allowed Moon to address 150,000 North Koreans, decided on an unprecedented visit to Seoul, and invited Pope Francis to Pyongyang. These gestures suggest that he may want to become North Korea's Deng Xiaoping. Yes, one cannot be too careful when dealing with the Kim regime; but nor should one be surprised that a young leader might pursue a different strategy from his father's.

Deng was able to concentrate on economic development only after diplomacy with the US had created a more favorable external environment for China. If there is even the slightest chance that Kim is serious about moving toward a normal state and a twenty-first century economy, the international community must not stand in his way. In that case, 2019 could be a year of continued progress toward a nuclear-free, peaceful Korean Peninsula. 🅿🆂

Yoon Young-kwan, former Minister of Foreign Affairs of the Republic of Korea, is Professor Emeritus of International Relations at Seoul National University.

1:
SOUTH KOREANS RALLY IN SUPPORT OF THE US-DPRK SUMMIT.

2:
SOLDIERS MARCH DURING THE 65TH SOUTH KOREA ARMED FORCES DAY.

3:
LIFE IN NORTH KOREA.

4:
YOUNG PEOPLE IN YEOUIDO PARK IN SEOUL.

The importance of peace and security has grown in significance in the recent years and the *Journal for Peace and Nuclear Disarmament**** serves as an important vehicle that puts forward proposals for policies and other ideas that could contribute to nuclear disarmament.

Browse
www.tandfonline.com/RPND

Taylor & Francis
Taylor & Francis Group

*The *Journal for Peace and Nuclear Disarmament* is an Open Access journal which means that all published research articles, interviews and discussions are free to access via the journal's homepage on Taylor & Francis Online.

NOT WORKING
Where Have All the Good Jobs Gone?
★ DAVID G. ★ BLANCHFLOWER

A candid assessment of why the job market is not as healthy we think

Cloth $29.95 | £24.00
Forthcoming June 2019

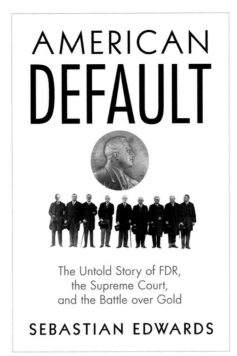

AMERICAN DEFAULT
The Untold Story of FDR, the Supreme Court, and the Battle over Gold
SEBASTIAN EDWARDS

"A superb history of the US exit from gold . . . satisfyingly detailed and highly accessible."
—David Frum

Cloth $29.95 | £24.00

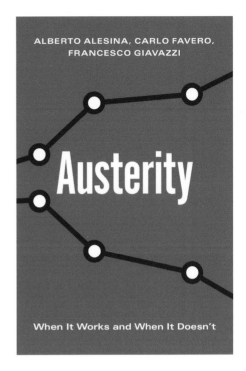

ALBERTO ALESINA, CARLO FAVERO, FRANCESCO GIAVAZZI

Austerity
When It Works and When It Doesn't

"An amazing, important, and timely book by leading thinkers on matters of fiscal policy."
—Harald Uhlig, University of Chicago

Cloth $35.00 | £27.00
Forthcoming February 2019

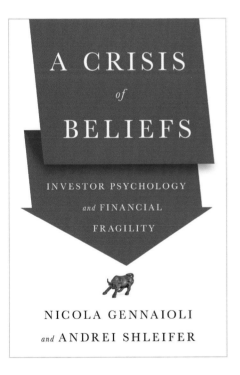

A CRISIS of BELIEFS
INVESTOR PSYCHOLOGY and FINANCIAL FRAGILITY
NICOLA GENNAIOLI and ANDREI SHLEIFER

"A milestone in the history of behavioral economics."
—Daniel Kahneman, winner of the 2002 Nobel Prize in economics, author of Thinking, Fast and Slow

Cloth $29.95 | £24.00

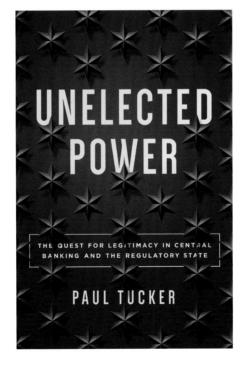

UNELECTED POWER
THE QUEST FOR LEGITIMACY IN CENTRAL BANKING AND THE REGULATORY STATE
PAUL TUCKER

"[Unelected Power] is of fundamental importance to anyone interested in the future of liberal democracy."
—Felix Martin, New Statesman

Cloth $35.00 | £27.00

How Growth REALLY Happens
The Making of Economic Miracles through Production, Governance, and Skills
Michael H. Best

"This book will profoundly change the way we see the economy. A masterpiece."
—Ha-Joon Chang, author of Economics: The User's Guide

Cloth $29.95 | £24.00

 PRINCETON UNIVERSITY PRESS

JEAN-CLAUDE JUNCKER
*President of the
European Commission*

The World Needs

Europe

As we usher in a new year, the future direction of the European Union has never been more important, both for Europe and for the rest of the world. In these increasingly tumultuous times, the EU can provide the stability and hope that the world so desperately needs. →

For decades, Europe has been the poster child for integration and cooperation in a fractured world. Since the end of World War II, the continent has been living proof that multilateralism works. Europe's troubled past has given way to a peace spanning seven decades, and to a Union of 500 million citizens living in freedom and prosperity. By any metric, Europe is now the most tolerant, free, and equal place to live anywhere in the world.

But the EU is not a given. Peace is not inevitable, and war is not implausible. The year 2018 marked the centenary of the end of World War I, the lessons of which must still be heeded. The Europeans of 1913 thought that war was impossible, that they were too interlinked to turn on one another. We Europeans have a rich tradition of ignoring premonitions of ruin at our own peril.

Given this history, today's reemergence of a dangerous brand of nationalism should be sounding alarm bells across our continent. I believe we owe it to generations past, present, and future to fight unchecked nationalism with all our might.

That means getting our own house in order, particularly on the economic front, by boosting investment through new forms of public and private partnerships. Moreover, to reduce risk across the EU, we need to fix our banking sector. That means shoring up a strong and stable eurozone, and deepening the Economic and Monetary Union. It also means not waiting for the next crisis to hit, but rather working proactively to make the EU more united and democratic than ever before.

Moreover, fighting nationalism at home means taking our destiny into our own hands. And yet, in a globalized world, Europe cannot secure its interests and values by itself. From migration and security to new technologies and ecological pressures, the collective challenges we face are multiplying by the day. As the divisions within societies and between countries deepen, the imperative to work together grows stronger.

By cooperating with friends from around the world, Europe's member states can become more resilient, both individually and collectively. Now is the time to offer

> **"What the world needs now is fairness and progress. The world needs Europe."**

1.

1:
THE EIFFEL TOWER ILLUMINATED WITH THE EU FLAG.

2:
EMMANUEL MACRON AT THE FIFTH AFRICAN UNION – EUROPEAN UNION SUMMIT.

2.

responsible global leadership. Now is the time to renew and redefine the ties that bind countries around the world, much as we are doing within our Union. Our brand of leadership is not about putting "Europe First." Rather, it is about being the first to answer the call for leadership when it matters.

Europe continues to set a global example as a region upholding the value of global solidarity. In 2016, Europe offered asylum to three times as many refugees as the United States, Canada, and Australia combined. And for years, Europe has provided more than half of the world's development and humanitarian aid.

For Europe, responsible global leadership also means setting fair standards. Only by putting people and their rights at the heart of the brave new digital world can we ensure that technological progress serves our people, as well as our planet. Whether it be brokering the Paris climate agreement, negotiating a deal with Iran to suspend its nuclear program, ridding our oceans of harmful plastic, or setting data protection standards, the EU is leading the charge on addressing the world's most pressing problems.

Cooperation, after all, is in our DNA. Individual European countries simply do not have the clout to shape global affairs on their own, and that is not going to change. By 2060, no single European country will have more than 1% of the world's population. Europeans must therefore continue to pool and share their national sovereignty, with the goal of establishing a stronger common sovereignty for all. As members of the world's largest single market – one that accounts for one-fifth of the global economy – each EU country is better placed to defend its national interests and to shape global events than it would be alone.

Looking ahead, our task is to strengthen this European sovereignty even further. That means speaking with one voice, sticking to our values, and delivering for our citizens ahead of the European Parliament election in May 2019.

History does not repeat itself, but it often rhymes. The world has been fractured before, and we have seen how this can lead to poverty, discord, and war. Europeans know – or should know – this pattern all too well. So we must fight the populists of this world, those who peddle the false hope of new dawns and those who replace fact with fiction and conjure "enemies" old and new.

Europe must provide the counterweight to these tendencies, by demonstrating that we can still champion compromise and consensus over the politics of strongmen. What the world needs now is fairness and progress. The world needs Europe. **PS**

Jean-Claude Juncker is President of the European Commission.

SHAPING EUROPE'S PRESENT AND FUTURE

AN INTERVIEW WITH FEDERICA MOGHERINI
EU High Representative for Foreign Affairs and Security Policy

CONDUCTED BY MARK LEONARD
Director of the European Council on Foreign Relations

1.

As the High Representative of the European Union for Foreign Affairs and Security Policy, Federica Mogherini has overseen EU foreign and security policy since November 2014. With her term coming to an end in 2019, Mark Leonard of the European Council on Foreign Relations asked Mogherini about the state of European security, the future of the international order, arms control, migration, and a broad range of other issues.

Mark Leonard: So far, the European Union has demonstrated an ability to maintain its unity over key issues like Brexit and the maintenance of the post-Crimea sanctions on Russia. Is this unity likely to hold in 2019, particularly given the looming EU parliamentary elections and changes at the top of the European Commission and Council?

Federica Mogherini: The unity of our Union is much stronger than often perceived. What I see in my daily work is an EU that makes decisions jointly, implements them together, and – especially in the field of foreign and security policy – acts as one. Many complain about the lack of unity. But my impression is that these complaints derive more from a comfortable cliché that is repeated on the basis of past experiences, rather than from a realistic reflection on the situation today.

Obviously, we need to define what we mean by "unity." It doesn't mean uniformity. We number 28 – soon 27, which is still a lot. With 500 million people, the EU is the largest integration project ever realized. The EU is the biggest market in the world, and the second-largest economy. It comprises many different cultures, languages, and politics. History and geography have given us different backgrounds. It is only natural that this translates into different views, opinions, voices – even within each of our democratic societies.

I have always refused to use the expression "the European Union must sing with one voice." We need to use all the different voices we have, because our plurality is our point of strength. But we need to sing the same song, in a coordinated manner, like a choir. And in my daily work, I see unity of purpose, common decisions, and coordinated action happening. I don't see this trend being challenged.

On the Brexit negotiations, the remaining 27 member states are more united than ever; and the decisions on sanctions with respect to Crimea have been taken, implemented, and renewed unanimously all these years. There are many other examples. Because we share the same interests as Europeans, I believe our citizens realize that – beyond slogans – the only effective way to achieve our objectives is to work together.

ML: You have called for Europe to defend its sovereignty by, for example, creating new structures that would allow it to continue to adhere to the Joint Comprehensive Plan of Action (JCPOA) with Iran. Will these structures actually work, and could the special-purpose vehicle to maintain trade with Iran be used to counter other US sanctions?

FM: We are working, as a Union of 28 member states and with the rest of the international community, to preserve a nuclear agreement that has so far been implemented in full, as certified by the International Atomic Energy Agency in 13 consecutive reports. We do this because of our collective security: we do not want to see Iran developing a nuclear weapon, and the JCPOA is delivering precisely on that purpose. I start by saying this because I often hear that, on this issue, Europe is motivated mainly by economic or trade considerations. That is not the case: we do this to prevent a nuclear non-proliferation agreement that is working from being dismantled, and to prevent a major security crisis in the Middle East.

Part of this work requires us to guarantee that firms wanting to do legitimate business with Iran are allowed to do so. This is what we are working on right now: tools that will assist, protect, and reassure economic actors pursuing legitimate business with Iran. It is true that this situation has triggered a conversation on European economic sovereignty. We Europeans cannot accept that a foreign power – even our closest friend and ally – makes decisions over our legitimate trade with another country. This is a basic element of sovereignty, and it is only natural that this reflection takes place, not only in Europe but in other parts of the world, too.

ML: The US decision to withdraw from the Intermediate-Range Nuclear Forces Treaty (INF) is a clear sign that US-Russia relations are as strained as at any time in three decades. So far, Europe has been unable to take decisive steps to defend the global disarmament order. What can the EU do to maintain nuclear stability in Europe, and to avoid the resumption of a missile race on the continent?

FM: The INF contributed to the end of the Cold War – and no one in Europe wants to go back to those dark days. Europe was the battlefield of superpowers, and we all lived under the constant threat of a nuclear war. Preventing a new arms race is in our collective interest. That is why we have asked the United States to consider the consequences its possible withdrawal from the INF will have on its own security, and on our collective security. And, we expect the Russian Federation to address serious concerns regarding its compliance with the INF. The current disarmament and non-proliferation architecture needs to become more universal, as a guarantee for all.

1:
IRANIAN NUCLEAR TALKS IN VIENNA.

2:
TURKISH PRESIDENT RECEP TAYYIP ERDOĞAN.

3:
RONALD REAGAN AND MIKHAIL GORBACHEV
AT THE SIGNING OF THE INF.

We Europeans are working at all levels to promote the universalization of existing agreements, such as the International Code of Conduct against Ballistic Missile Proliferation. The starting point cannot be to dismantle the current architecture and start from scratch. That is a risk that nobody can afford. Non-proliferation is a field where it is essential to exercise collective responsibility, as the stakes are too high for all.

ML: Five years after the invasion of Crimea and the outbreak of fighting in eastern Ukraine, peace in that country seems as far away as ever. What, if anything, can Europe do to dampen the prospects of renewed violence, and will the EU remain united in its position toward Russia, particularly concerning sanctions?

FM: Peace in eastern Ukraine is something that the EU continues to work for every day. The sanctions are part of a broader framework. We have mobilized the biggest-ever assistance package from the EU to any country – almost €14 billion ($16 billion) since 2014. This also includes specific support to the Organization for Security and Cooperation in Europe's Special Monitoring Mission, and an EU Advisory Mission that is working on civilian security-sector reform.

We are focusing, in particular, on local governance and local development in the east of the country. And we are following discussions at the United Nations on a possible UN peacekeeping mission, although there hasn't been much progress on that in recent months. I expect the economic sanctions to remain in place, because the reasons for imposing them – to advance the full implementation of the Minsk Agreements and restore Ukraine's territorial integrity – still stand.

ML: Can more be done to deter Russia from interfering in European elections?

FM: There are a number of actions we are taking to guard against the challenge of external interference, no matter where it may come from: building up our cybersecurity capacities; improving the protection of personal data; guaranteeing the transparency of online political advertising; and improving cooperation among EU member states, and with our global partners.

We have also made it possible to introduce sanctions for cyberattacks, which sends a strong message that such hostile ➡

activity will not be tolerated and will have serious consequences. There is another strand of work, however, which needs to be reinforced, and that is empowering our citizens to make informed democratic choices. This is the best way to protect our democracies from all sorts of disinformation.

ML: Europe now often seems to be the last big voice defending the liberal international order and open trading system. What can it do to encourage China, India, and other powers to make a firmer commitment to the liberal order?

FM: First of all, we must guarantee the highest standards inside our Union, to keep our own societies open, respectful, and free. It is a matter of conformity with our values, but also of credibility in our external action. Beyond that, this is indeed a crucial moment to protect and advance a more cooperative and multilateral global order. Many powers around the world want to cooperate with the EU to preserve open markets and to make global institutions fit for our multipolar world. We don't all share the same principles and values: we know these are tough times in terms of human rights in many parts of the world. But the best way we have to promote human rights – or a fairer form of globalization – is through engagement with all interlocutors.

We are the only power that engages in regular human-rights dialogue in all corners of the world. And our new generation of trade agreements includes strong protections for workers' rights, intellectual property, and the environment. They are agreements for free and fair trade. This is the time for the EU to place itself at the center of a network of likeminded partners around the world, one that promotes and strengthens multilateralism and a rules-based international order.

ML: Why has Europe's weight in its neighborhood decreased, especially when it comes to shaping events in Turkey, Libya, and Syria? Is this an indication that Europe will not be one of the great powers of the twenty-first century?

FM: Our destiny is in our own hands. If we want to play a decisive role, not only in our region but also globally, we have all the right instruments to do so – and we have the weight to do so. Let me add that this is also what our partners around the world expect from us, particularly in these difficult times. To play such a role, Europeans need to realize how big and powerful they are when they act together as a Union, and focus more on the responsibility we can exercise on the global scene if we resist the temptation of inward-looking policies – or rather, politics.

Our greatest enemy is a lack of trust in the means at our disposal. The EU has unparalleled "soft" power – in economic, diplomatic, and cultural terms – and we are increasingly active as a global security provider, building our "hard" power as never before. In Syria and Libya, we are not a military player – and I am proud of this. Violence has brought more violence, while we have always worked for peaceful and negotiated solutions.

Does this mean we are powerless? Quite the contrary. At the UN General Assembly this year, more than 50 countries and organizations took part in the discussion we initiated on Syria, to support the difficult work the UN is doing there. Everyone understands that the EU's role in Syria and Libya is unique and irreplaceable: we talk to all parties and are an honest broker and indispensable partner in the effort to ensure peace, security, and stabilization. Too often, we do not realize our own potential and power. Our partners sometimes see it more clearly than Europeans do.

ML: What impact will Britain's exit from the EU have on the EU's security strategy? Will it help forge a stronger consensus?

FM: I have no doubt that our future is one of close partnership and cooperation. If you look at what has happened since the Brexit referendum in 2016, we are still making unanimous decisions on foreign, security, and defense policies: we reacted as one to the nerve-agent attack in Salisbury, England, earlier this year; we continue to work together when it comes to preserving the Iran nuclear deal; and we are pursuing shared objectives in Ukraine, Syria, Afghanistan, Myanmar, and elsewhere.

In the coming months, I will present a proposal for a new way of collaborating with non-EU countries and international organizations that are involved in EU civilian and military operations, or that are otherwise associated with our security and defense policies. This will also be an essential part of our future relationship with the UK. We will seek ways ➡

1:
A PRO-RUSSIA SEPARATIST
AT DONETSK AIRPORT.

for non-EU countries to participate in defense projects launched under the Permanent Structured Cooperation (PESCO) framework.

ML: The Franco-German engine has long been seen as essential to formulating and implementing successful EU policies, both internal and external. For years, it was said that Germany was waiting for an effective French partner. In French President Emmanuel Macron, the Germans appear to have one, but Germany itself, afflicted with a kind of political paralysis, now seems to be turning inward. Where do you see Franco-German relations headed in the year ahead?

FM: European integration was originally driven by the Franco-German engine, but it has always been a much larger project. Its strength has always been its attractiveness. Two years ago, when we decided to take some unprecedented steps toward establishing a "Europe of Defense," I was immediately supported by the defense ministers of four countries: France, Germany, Italy, and Spain. But less than a year later, as many as 25 member states had agreed to launch PESCO. When the benefits of cooperation and integration are clear, when the added value of our Union is self-evident, all EU member states focus on their common interest and move forward together.

ML: What do you believe foreign policy can and should do to fight populism?

FM: I don't like the expression "populism." I believe a lot of people have lost trust in the institutions – all of them. But in most European countries, the EU is more trusted than national institutions. The reaction coming from some political forces is to shift the blame and find a scapegoat. Governments come to Brussels, make decisions by unanimity, and then blame the results on the EU. But the Union is what we make of it. We have a collective responsibility to make it work. It is a reflection of our own collective political will.

In these past few years, our foreign policy has advanced and protected European citizens' interests and values in a way that no member state could have achieved alone. In today's world, even the "bigger" member states are small, such that national sovereignty can be effectively exercised only through the EU. We show this every day in our foreign policy. We are more effective at negotiating trade

1.

deals as the world's largest market than as 28 separate countries. We have a bigger impact when we address climate change collectively than we would if each country moved at its own pace. We see the benefits of cooperating among ourselves when it comes to enhancing security in our partner countries. We are stronger and much more effective together.

Those who want to dismantle or weaken the EU are trying to weaken the most powerful instrument we Europeans have to exercise our sovereignty. This might be in the interest of our competitors in the world, but it is definitely not in the interest of European citizens.

ML: If there is a populist surge in the upcoming European Parliament elections, what lessons should Brussels take from it, and what new course would you advocate?

FM: Whatever the result of the election, the lessons will have to be taken not so much "in Brussels" but everywhere around the Union, and most of all in member states' capitals. EU policies and actions are defined through our collective work, which is the result of our political will. If it works, it is a collective success for all of us; if it fails, it is a collective responsibility, and a problem for all. No one is excluded.

The EU is not a building in Brussels. It is a project of 500 million citizens, their national governments, the parliamentary members they elect to represent them, and the European Commission that those MEPs elect. I personally believe that Europeans need their Union, and need to change some of the policies that the EU has put in place. This is something we have begun to do in recent years: deepening European integration on security and defense; establishing a strong and united external policy to govern migration flows; and launching the largest-ever investment plan for Europe and Africa.

Some want to change EU policies to improve them – even radically – but others just want to destroy the Union. We have to be very careful, because in times of frustration, destruction can sound fascinating for many. And yet the secret of change is to focus not on destroying the old, but on building the new. I hope this will be possible in 2019.

ML: At your European Parliament talk with Microsoft co-founder Bill Gates in October, you spoke about the need for the EU to be "generously selfish" in its future relationship with Africa. Can you explain how you see this working in practice? What's the right balance between sacrificing values and dampening the desire to migrate?

FM: This is not about sacrificing our values – in fact, the exact opposite is true. We must realize that our interests and values coincide. Our values tell us that all people should have the right to follow their dreams and aspirations, to contribute to their countries' public life, and to live free from fear. Too many Africans do not enjoy these rights, and this is hampering Africa's immense potential.

We Europeans have an interest in a stronger Africa, because that will also make Europe stronger. In practice, this means that Africa needs more jobs, better education, stronger democracies, sustainable development, and a more stable security environment. The decision to leave your home country is never easy. Africa's youth would like to find the opportunities they seek within their home countries. They would like to change their countries' economies and political systems, instead of changing countries altogether. This is what the Africans are asking us: to work with them, so that they can help Africa realize its huge potential.

ML: Do recent developments in the EU's external approach to migration in places like Africa and the Middle East signal a move away from "emergency responses" and toward long-term solutions?

FM: Not just the recent developments. This has been the goal of our external action on migration since the very beginning. Let me remind you of the situation three years ago: hundreds of people were dying almost every day in the Mediterranean and in the North African desert. Until then, the EU had been indifferent to a phenomenon that it considered to be outside its competence and under the exclusive purview of individual member states.

This has changed, finally. We had to create an emergency response to end the carnage, and we did it with Operation Sophia at sea and the Emergency Trust Fund to finance our work with Africa. At the same time, we started to work on a better system to manage migration flows and address their long-term causes. We started to train local security forces; we worked on voluntary returns for migrants, with the opportunity to start a new life; and we established our investment plan for Africa and Europe's neighborhood.

Today, I believe we all understand that the right approach is to forge partnerships with countries of origin and transit, and with organizations such as the UN and the African Union. Today we must change course on the internal policies governing migration and introduce a principle of solidarity among Europeans that is currently still very much opposed by some member states. At the same time, we must continue on the same path with our external policies on migration. That means getting more investment from member states, avoiding U-turns, and doing much more to open safe and regular pathways for human mobility.

ML: You have been involved in episodes and negotiations affecting the course of global affairs. Are there any that you would like to revisit?

FM: In my job, the important thing is to look forward, rather than to look back. It sounds obvious, but that is how things work. You cannot change the past; you can only focus on shaping the present and the future. That means having ambitious but realistic objectives, and building partnerships to try to achieve them together with others, in a cooperative manner.

ML: As you complete your term as EU High Commissioner, what do you think are the top three examples of the added value of the European External Action Service, compared to the pre-Lisbon Treaty institutional setup?

FM: I remember the discussions from ten years ago, when the Lisbon Treaty was approved. Many believed that the High Representative would have an impossible job, with three "hats" – as vice president of the Commission, chair of the Foreign Affairs Council, and head of the European Defense Agency. In fact, the intuition behind that job description has been fully vindicated. The EU has an unparalleled set of foreign- and security-policy tools, and only with three hats is it possible to mobilize our foreign policy's full potential.

That means that I chair the meetings of foreign, defense, and development ministers. I take part in the European Council. I coordinate the group of commissioners dealing with external action. I work with our military and civilian personnel on security and defense issues. And I can rely on our remarkable diplomatic service, with talented professionals at headquarters and a network of 140 embassies around the world.

Without all of this, our work to build a "Europe of Defense" would not have been possible, and our strong partnership with Africa – starting with migration, but going well beyond that – would not exist. The same goes for the Iran nuclear deal, our trade agreements around the world, the dialogue between Serbia and Kosovo, and all the vital work we do with the Balkans to work for peace, reconciliation, regional integration, and economic development in the heart of Europe. **PS**

Federica Mogherini is High Representative of the European Union for Foreign Affairs and Security Policy and Vice President of the European Commission.

Mark Leonard is Director of the European Council on Foreign Relations.

1:
A TUNISIAN START-UP SUPPORTED BY THE EU AND THE EUROPEAN COMMITTEE FOR TRAINING AND AGRICULTURE.

2:
ITALY'S EUROSKEPTIC INTERIOR MINISTER MATTEO SALVINI.

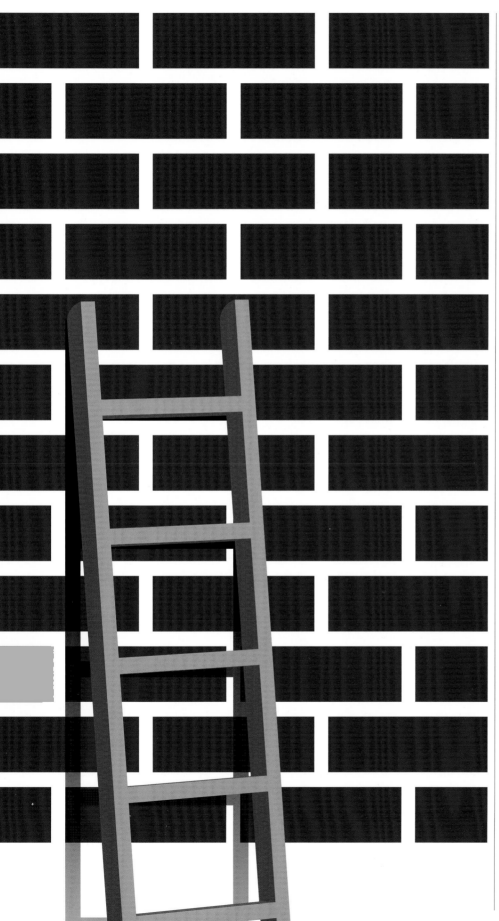

What Next for Global Trade?

PINELOPI KOUJIANOU GOLDBERG
Chief Economist of the World Bank

The year 2018 marked the return of the import tariff. As of October, the United States had imposed levies on roughly 12,000 products, accounting for 12.6% of its total imports; its main trading partners had retaliated with tariffs on 2,087 products, accounting for 6.2% of US exports. With trade tensions mounting, many observers have warned of a full-scale trade war, or even the collapse of the global trading system.

Of course, this is not the first time in recent history that the US has tried using trade policy to advance its interests. In 1971, the Nixon administration famously imposed a 10% tariff on *all* imports in an attempt to halt the growth of the US current-account deficit. And more recently, the Reagan administration erected non-tariff barriers against a number of import goods, particularly from Japan.

Nonetheless, there are some key differences between these episodes and the latest wave of tariff increases. For starters, the timing is surprising. Until 2018, globalization seemed like an unstoppable and irreversible force. International trade was considered to be completely liberalized, and any talk of trade policy was met with yawns in academic and policy circles alike. Stranger still, the rise of protectionism has come at a time when US ➡

AS OF OCTOBER 2018, THE US HAD IMPOSED TARIFFS ON ROUGHLY 12,000 PRODUCTS.

AMERICA'S MAIN TRADING PARTNERS HAVE IMPOSED TARIFFS ON 2,087 OF ITS PRODUCTS.

unemployment is at a 50-year low, the stock market is up, and GDP growth is projected to be around 3% for the year.

The opening salvo of tariff increases – on washing machines and solar panels – seemed to be geared toward protecting specific domestic industries that had been hurt by import competition. And these were soon accompanied by sweeping tariffs of 25% on steel and 10% on aluminum, as well as the renegotiation of the North American Free Trade Agreement (NAFTA). The latest wave has singled out China, presumably to address long-standing concerns about that country's treatment of intellectual property, restriction of market access, and subsidies for state-owned enterprises. (As for America's trading partners, each has responded in a way designed to inflict political damage on congressional Republicans.)

The recent US trade policy thus seems to be motivated by two key priorities: to protect US jobs in import-competing sectors, and to address frustrations with the current trading system that the World Trade Organization (WTO) has failed to resolve. It is this second motivation that makes the current bout of protectionism different – and potentially more dangerous – than other recent episodes.

After all, using trade policy to protect domestic jobs is not new, though it has fallen out of favor over time. Most policymakers now accept that a social safety net and domestic policies such as retraining or relocation subsidies are more effective responses to the displacement of workers in open, constantly evolving economies. The fact that NAFTA survived the renegotiation process with only minor modifications is a case in point.

The real issue, then, is the current trading system and its various shortcomings. In fact, the claim that trade has been completely liberalized in advanced economies is tenable only if one focuses solely on tariffs and ignores "behind the border" measures, which are substantially harder to measure, let alone address. These include regulatory restrictions that hinder cross-border investment; subsidies to domestic industries; licensing requirements that inhibit trade in services; privacy requirements that restrict e-commerce; restrictions on foreign ownership that interfere with inward direct investment; and stringent joint-venture requirements that often

entail handing over intellectual property. If there is one area of wide agreement across countries and political parties, it is that cross-border transactions and regulation leave a lot to be desired.

In principle, these issues should have been addressed through multilateral negotiations at the WTO. In practice, they have been dealt with in an *ad hoc* fashion, through a slow, overly bureaucratic process that has failed to get to the root of the problem.

The medium- and long-term effects of today's trade disputes remain to be seen. Simulations based on computational general equilibrium models predict that the current tariff increases will have a small impact on the US and a slightly larger impact on China. And in the case of a "full-scale" trade war – meaning 25% tariffs on all Chinese imports to the US, and vice versa – the effects would be slightly larger, but by no means catastrophic.

The greater danger is that today's policy shifts will continue to create uncertainty, thus reducing investment. Scholars have repeatedly shown that overall investment is highly sensitive to changes in perception regarding the economic environment. For example, studies have found that investment in a given locality can even be affected by the victory or loss of a local sports team. Now consider the current situation, in which there is growing uncertainty about the future of the rules-based trading system and global value chains. Needless to say, the effect on investment could be chilling indeed.

Moreover, while large economies like the US and China will survive the current contretemps – albeit with bruises – smaller emerging economies have much more to lose. For many of these smaller economies, trade has been the ticket out of poverty. By adhering to the common rules of the WTO, they managed to keep domestic lobbies and special interests at bay and develop economically. Were the multilateral trading system to collapse, protectionist interests around the world would suddenly have little standing in their way.

An optimistic view of the current situation is that it will bring countries to the negotiating table, eventually leading to a more effective multilateral system. Such a system might include a reformed WTO; trade liberalization in services and e-commerce; agreements limiting

> **For those concerned about the future of trade, the only certainty about the year ahead is that it will be a nail-biter.**

subsidies and protecting intellectual property; and deeper cross-border regulatory coordination.

An optimist cannot help but draw parallels to the 1980s, when the global trading system was challenged by rising tensions between the US and Japan. Rather than collapsing, the trading system emerged from those disputes stronger than before, setting the stage for the hyper-globalization of the last three decades. Perhaps a similar future for international trade lies ahead.

Or perhaps not. For those concerned about the future of trade, the only certainty about the year ahead is that it will be a nail-biter. PS

Pinelopi Koujianou Goldberg is World Bank Group Chief Economist, Professor of Economics at Yale University, and a former editor-in-chief of the American Economic Review.

1:
WORKERS IN CHINA'S EASTERN ANHUI PROVINCE.

1.

The Right Way to Rebalance Trade

ZHU MIN
Former Deputy Managing Director of the IMF

MIAO YANLIANG
Chief Economist at China's State Administration for Foreign Exchange

The US-China trade dispute reshaped the world's economic and financial landscape in 2018, and it might continue to do so for years to come. That's not how it looked as recently as May, when a bilateral trade deal was almost within reach. But the United States backed out at the eleventh hour, and tensions have since flared, with President Donald Trump's administration imposing tariffs on a wide range of Chinese exports, and China responding in kind.

With an unprecedented $600 billion worth of goods potentially affected, it is worth considering how useful tariffs really are for correcting current-account imbalances, which is Trump's stated goal. Most economists view trade from a multilateral perspective, focusing on an economy's overall balance with the rest of the world. And the US has been running overall trade deficits since 1976.

The US deficit peaked at 5.5% of GDP in 2006, but usually amounts to around 3% of GDP. At $552 billion in 2017, it is the world's largest deficit in absolute terms. Deficits rise when a country spends more than it produces, which means that they are rooted not so much in trade as in domestic savings and investment behavior. In the US, investment accounts for 21% of GDP, in keeping with the average across advanced economies (22%), whereas savings account for less than 19%, which is far below that of America's peers.

The US saving rate reflects both public- and private-sector behavior. The personal saving rate was as low as 3% in the run-up to the 2008 financial crisis, after which it edged up to 7% – a rate still far below that of the early 1990s. Meanwhile, the public sector has historically saved even less. The US has had a federal budget surplus in only five of the last 50 years, and it has maintained deficits averaging more than 4% of GDP since 2002. In 2018, the deficit rose by 17% on the back of tax cuts and increased defense spending, further dampening public savings.

Underlying the low US saving rate is the dollar's status as the main global reserve currency. The dollar's dominance confers on America what Valéry Giscard D'Estaing, then France's finance minister, famously dubbed an "exorbitant privilege," insofar as it allows the US to finance its deficits with little external constraint, borrowing ever more from abroad while saving less at home. By the end of 2017, foreigners owned half of the $12 trillion worth of privately held US Treasury securities that are currently outstanding.

As the multilateral perspective makes clear, the US current-account deficit can be reduced only through structural reforms to address the imbalance between domestic savings and investment. Such reforms have become all the more urgent with the unchecked growth of entitlement spending, and with US unilateralism on trade now testing global confidence in the dollar. ➲

US TRADE DEFICIT IN 2017.

$552B

19%
SAVINGS IN THE US
(% OF GDP).

22%
SAVINGS IN PEER COUNTRIES
(% OF GDP).

$12 TRILLION
OUTSTANDING US TREASURY SECURITIES
OWNED BY THE PUBLIC.

Notwithstanding these economic realities, the Trump administration has embraced a bilateral perspective. Its tariffs on Chinese exports are meant to improve the US trade balance *vis-à-vis* China specifically. But if the US imports less from China, it will simply import more from other countries. Its overall trade deficit will likely remain the same or grow even larger, as the latest data suggest.

Worse still, tariffs come with far-reaching costs. As the American economist Henry George observed 132 years ago, "What protection teaches us is to do to ourselves in time of peace what enemies seek to do to us in time of war." Indeed, history is filled with cases of high tariffs turning economic slumps into major depressions. And even at a time of growth, the Trump administration's tariffs will not just force Americans to pay more for imports; they will also undermine US production, by distorting business incentives and misallocating resources. Moreover, tariffs are hard to reverse, because they breed special interests and invite retaliation.

Yet, despite their high long-term costs, tariffs are addictive as a political device, because they allow governments to offer short-term sweeteners instead of more difficult structural reforms. But even if politicians are willing to turn a blind eye to the risks of protectionism, markets will not, as evidenced by the volatility in US stock markets in October 2018.

As for China, its adherence to the multilateral perspective on trade has led it to reduce its external imbalance through structural reforms. Unlike the US, China has had too much saving and too little spending. But in the decade since the global financial crisis, it has introduced policies to narrow the urban-rural income gap and strengthen the social safety net, thereby boosting consumption and reducing saving.

Such reforms have brought China's current-account surplus down from nearly 10% to 1% of GDP over the past decade. In the first three quarters of 2018, final consumption expenditure accounted for nearly 80% of Chinese GDP growth, reflecting the fact that the economy is increasingly driven by domestic demand. By actively reducing its external surplus, China has demonstrated that it is not a mercantilist power, but rather a responsible global stakeholder pursuing balanced and sustainable long-term growth.

1.

1:
CHINESE PRESIDENT XI JINPING.

Looking ahead, China should continue to pursue structural reforms that open up its economy, not least by improving intellectual-property protection and creating a level playing field for competition between domestic and foreign firms. Such goals are firmly in line with the objective of balanced, sustainable growth.

To be sure, China has been accused of merely paying lip service to openness, particularly by foreign investors who have found it difficult to enter the Chinese market. The real problem, however, is not a lack of commitment to reform, but rather administrative red tape, which domestic constituents also complain about. Recent measures, such as the "one stop, one trip, one paper" program in Zhejiang province, demonstrate that China is serious about improving the business environment for all.

Whether the multilateral perspective prevails over the bilateral approach will have significant consequences over the medium and long term. Obviously, the multilateral view offers a better understanding of trade imbalances than the bilateral perspective, just as structural reforms are a better alternative than tariffs. At the end of the day, external imbalances can be addressed only by correcting domestic imbalances. Because China has embraced this principle, its economy will continue to become more balanced and sustainable, regardless of the path the US chooses. PS

Zhu Min, *a former Deputy Managing Director of the IMF, is Chair of the National Institute of Financial Research at Tsinghua University.*

Miao Yanliang, *Chief Economist at China's State Administration for Foreign Exchange, has been a member of the China Finance 40 Forum since 2015.*

The Future of Free Trade

MICHAEL FROMAN
Former US Trade Representative

In 2018, trade, more than any other policy area, was "disrupted." What used to be an archaic, technical, and – let's face it – boring array of issues now dominates front-page headlines, magazine covers, and even John Oliver's comedic documentaries on HBO's "Last Week Tonight." Constituencies that have traditionally opposed free-trade agreements (FTAs) are now extolling their virtues, and countries not known for their free-trade sensibilities – including China, Russia, and France – are nominating themselves as the defenders of the global trade system.

Still, it is worth asking how much has actually been disrupted. President Donald Trump did pull the United States out of the 12-country Trans-Pacific Partnership (TPP), but the remaining 11 signatories have implemented the bulk of the agreement on their own, while leaving the door open for the US to rejoin in the future. And more countries have shown an interest in joining, suggesting that the TPP could eventually extend well beyond what was originally envisioned. Moreover, the updated North American Free Trade Agreement – now to be called the United States-Mexico-Canada Agreement – is largely based on the TPP template, which already included Canada and Mexico, with some noteworthy additions.

Meanwhile, the European Union is implementing FTAs with Canada, Singapore, Vietnam, and Japan, and pursuing deals with Australia, Mexico, New Zealand, the Association of Southeast Asian Nations, Mercosur, and others. The Pacific Alliance continues to expand trade and other partnerships in Latin America. The Regional Comprehensive Economic Partnership (RCEP) is proceeding apace in the Asia-Pacific region. And the African Union has made more progress toward implementing the Continental Free Trade Agreement (CFTA).

In short, the global trend toward deeper integration and higher standards in trade has continued. The Trump administration has certainly made a lot of noise by deploying trade remedies in unpredictable and unexpected ways, engaging in tit-for-tat tariffs, reintroducing import quotas, and seriously constraining the World Trade Organization's dispute-settlement body. Yet, in the end, Trump's revamping of NAFTA might actually help to broaden support for trade in the US, given ➡

> **But one thing is clear: nationalism, populism, nativism, and protectionism are on the rise.**

that many of his most loyal supporters have traditionally been suspicious of trade agreements.

That, at any rate, is the glass-half-full interpretation. The alternative is that there has, in fact, been a significant historical rupture. By surrendering its global leadership role, the US has lost the trust of its closest allies and partners, and handed a gift to its adversaries. In this scenario, the EU or China might supplant the US as the global rule-maker, or there will be no rule-maker, and the international order will be governed by drift. In the latter case, other countries might well imitate the US by pursuing unilateral action and upholding their international obligations only when it suits them.

It is too early to say which scenario will play out. But one thing is clear: nationalism, populism, nativism, and protectionism are on the rise. Economic insecurities, as well as a growing sense of lost sovereignty, have contributed to an unprecedented degree of political polarization, and not just in the US. From European countries beset by growth in support for fringe parties to emerging economies mired in corruption, governments everywhere seem to be more inwardly focused and less capable than ever of demonstrating bold leadership – and precisely when it is most needed to address the disruptive effects of rapid technological and economic change.

With a leadership vacuum at the international level and paralysis at the national level, it has become all the more necessary for private-sector actors to step up, not out of the goodness of their hearts, but in defense of their own interests. As BlackRock chairman and CEO Larry Fink and others have pointed out, it is no longer enough for companies to be focused solely on short-term returns to shareholders. They also need to be thinking about the long term and about the economic and political environments in which they operate. Beyond corporate social responsibility and philanthropy, both of which are important, that means developing commercially sustainable business models that also "serve a social purpose."

Doing well by doing good can't be just a tagline. It must be a guiding business philosophy, backed by the recognition that the private sector needs a healthy

1:
DOCK WORKER IN CHINA'S SHANDONG PROVINCE.

2:
WTO DIRECTOR-GENERAL ROBERTO AZEVEDO.

3:
KEY MEMBERS OF THE TRUMP TEAM CONGRATULATE ONE ANOTHER BEFORE PRESENTING THE REVISED USMCA TRADE AGREEMENT.

political and economic environment to thrive and must take action to secure it. In recent decades, public trust in government, the press, corporations, and other leading institutions has declined sharply. If business leaders continue to ignore the health of their operating environment – or assume that fixing it is someone else's problem – they are risking even more deglobalization, uncertainty, and instability in the years ahead.

Economic growth has been the defining feature of an historic global success story spanning the past 75 years. Even with its limitations, globalization has lifted more than one billion people out of poverty and delivered unprecedented improvements in virtually all areas of human development. But the job is not done. To prevent backsliding, the focus must shift from aggregate growth to inclusive growth. The gains from growth must accrue not just to those at the top, but to those at all income levels, and not just to global corporations, but to small and medium-size businesses as well.

Nationalism, populism, nativism, and protectionism exploit people's sense of being left behind and excluded from the system. That is why we need to focus on ensuring universal inclusion in the economic networks that allow individuals and families to achieve financial security and pursue opportunities for betterment. This imperative applies as much to a Kenyan farmer or an Egyptian garment worker as it does to an American now eking out a living in the gig economy.

It remains to be seen whether the current disruption in trade policy will be deep and long-lasting, or superficial and temporary. We cannot yet know if we will see a return to the mean or whether Pandora's box has been opened. But, in the absence of international and national leadership, businesses should not wait to find out. **P𝕊**

Michael Froman, US Trade Representative during President Barack Obama's administration, is Vice Chairman of Mastercard.

Trump's Trade Game

DANI RODRIK
*Professor, Harvard Kennedy
School of Government*

US President Donald Trump's "America first" trade policy came into full bloom in 2018, and it was an ugly sight to behold. In addition to tariffs on steel and aluminum from Europe and other countries, Trump imposed levies on $250 billion worth of imports from China. By the end of the year, he had raised tariffs on 12% of total US imports, causing trade partners to retaliate with levies on 8% of total US exports.

Trump's trade-policy unilateralism is unprecedented in the post-war period, which is why it caught many by surprise. I, for one, did not expect Trump to act on most of his threats, given the influence that commercial and financial interests have over US trade policy. But when the target is China, the situation changes. The Trump administration's tough approach is supported by a broad coalition of US groups with distinct grievances. These include not just traditionally protectionist lobbies, but also large corporations that bemoan China's industrial policies and a national-security establishment that frets over China's growing geopolitical footprint.

Trump's stated objective is to pressure China to end "unfair" trade practices, such as its subsidies for new technologies and its requirement that foreign companies entering the domestic market transfer proprietary technology to Chinese firms. So far, he has had little success, and that isn't likely to change. Understandably, the Chinese government will not be deterred from pursuing its own objectives of industrial upgrading and technological development.

Still, Trump did clinch one superficial victory in 2018, by concluding the renegotiation of the North American Free Trade Agreement with Canada and Mexico. Trump has heralded the revised NAFTA – renamed the United States-Mexico-Canada Agreement (USMCA) – as "historic," "the most advanced trade deal in the world," and "a new model for US trade relations." In reality, the changes to the deal are relatively minor, and amount to a mixed bag of pluses and minuses. Above all, they expose the fundamental incoherence of Trump's larger trade agenda.

> **The deeper – and arguably bigger – cost of Trump's trade policies is that they will distract us from addressing real flaws in the global trade regime.**

On the positive side, the new agreement strengthens environmental and labor standards somewhat, and limits foreign investors' standing to sue host governments in international tribunals. But the impact of these revisions is unclear. For example, investors can still bring claims under the original NAFTA rules for up to three years after the USMCA has gone into force. As one pro-investor website puts it, "United States investors in Mexico and in Canada who have a potential claim should seriously consider availing themselves of NAFTA protections while they still can."

While Trump has nominally reduced protections for US corporations in one area, he has increased them in others. For starters, the new deal has much more restrictive rules of origin, meaning that a larger share of automotive inputs will have to be manufactured in North America to qualify for tariff exemptions. Also, a first-ever wage floor has been imposed: by 2023, 40-45% of car and truck components will have to be produced by workers earning at least $16 per hour. This provision effectively prices a large chunk of supply chains out of Mexico, where wages are a small fraction of the floor.

Less noticed are the novel protections that pharmaceutical and technology companies have received under the guise of modernizing the agreement. Under the USMCA, both Canada and Mexico will have to make patent terms – including data-protection terms in biologics – more restrictive in order to align with the US. And governments are barred from requiring digital firms to localize computing facilities, as well as from interfering in the cross-border transfer of data and personal information.

Though Trump's unilateralism and mercantilism are bad for the world economy, one should not exaggerate the adverse effects of his administration's approach. If other countries do not overreact – and, so far, they have not – the consequences for world trade will remain manageable. After all, the global trade slowdown predates Trump, and is rooted in ongoing structural and technological trends: the shift in global demand from goods to (less tradable) services; the increased skill-intensity of manufacturing, which weakens offshoring incentives; automation and the consequent reshoring of supply chains; and China's transition from export-led to domestic-demand-led growth. Collectively, these developments are likely to have a larger impact on trade than Trump's bluster ever could.

The deeper – and arguably bigger – cost of Trump's trade policies is that they will distract us from addressing real flaws in the global trade regime. As is always the case with Trump, the challenge is not to lose sight of the genuine grievances that he has tapped. The more outrageous Trump's actions, the greater the risk that mainstream policy elites will rally behind the flawed *ancien régime*.

Recall that when Trump was elected in November 2016, trade technocrats and international bureaucrats responded by acknowledging that hyper-globalization had left many people behind. There was genuine soul-searching about the need for more robust compensatory mechanisms and other remedies. But such talk has since all but disappeared. These days, one hears all about the virtues of the liberal, multilateral trading system, and almost nothing about the severe imbalances it has created.

And yet we desperately need a new vision for world trade. Existing rules are not up to the challenge of accommodating countries like China, where economic practices are very different from those of the US or Europe. Moreover, the current system provides neither safeguards for maintaining high labor standards in advanced economies, nor adequate measures to prevent regulatory and tax arbitrage.

Trump's antics present us with a false choice between supporting his approach and defending the old rules. If we are genuinely committed to ensuring that globalization benefits all, we must not play his game.

***Dani Rodrik**, Professor of International Political Economy at Harvard University's John F. Kennedy School of Government, is the author of* Straight Talk on Trade: Ideas for a Sane World Economy.

AI and the Challenge of Culture

JAMES CARNEY
Texture AI

We have a technology for making imaginary things real – it's called culture. Culture is how the past talks to the present, and the present to the future. Every value we have, every desire we express, is mediated by culture. Were we to be visited by an alien species, the first thing they would wish to know about is our culture. Culture is not something you experience; culture is something you are.

From one perspective, this is a golden age of culture: never before have the products of human creativity been available in such abundance and with such ease. But from another perspective, our grasp on culture has never been so shallow. We take something that is plural and subtle and reduce it to a single dimension of variance – whether or not we *like* it. Or we identify culture with how many people it reaches, rather than with the effects it has.

If this is error, it is error of a particularly egregious kind. And that's because the biggest innovation in cognition since the invention of language – machine learning and artificial intelligence – is now being trained on bad cultural data. It's one thing to have a poor model of, say, cardboard box manufacturing; it's another issue entirely to misrepresent systematically the core activity of being human.

And we already know the results. Chatbots learn hate speech overnight; programmatic servers issue threats of violence as ads. Classifiers make racist identifications; decision trees systematically discriminate against specific groups. This is what happens when critical, informed models of cultural processes are replaced with glib, facile metrics that contain as much noise as

> **But there remains a body of models that give us real insight into how human beings create and engage with culture.**

they do data. And it's just the beginning of what will happen as algorithmic learning comes to play an ever-greater role in automating our lives.

The point is not to refuse AI and machine learning. These technologies have already proved their value in areas like health care, scientific research, defense, and education. They are here to stay. The point, instead, is to register that applying these technologies to culture is qualitatively different from applying them to physical processes. Doing so successfully will require a level of sophistication in the analysis of culture that is simply not yet evident in the technology sector.

How do we create representations of culture that are adequate to its richness? The answer comes after recognizing that this is not the first time the question has been asked. In 1871, E.B. Tylor defined culture as "that complex whole which includes knowledge, belief, art, morals, law, custom, and any other capabilities and habits acquired by man as a member of society," and with that, launched the discipline of cultural anthropology. Since then, the intellectual understanding of how culture functions has been a core project of the humanities and social sciences.

Sometimes, the models of culture that are developed are unusable, or unsupported by the data, or simply vehicles for the political opinions of their originators. But there remains a body of models that give us real insight into how human beings create and engage with culture. We have, for example, robust accounts of how culture interacts with human psychology to create structured knowledge. We know how culture combines discrete cognitive tools into patterns of religious thought and behavior. We have a good grasp of how mid-level cultural structures like stories, genres, and rituals work. We now understand how cognitive constraints affect the spread of cultural representations over time and space. Such insights are the outcome of generations of patient scholarship that engages with the inner working of culture.

Algorithmic implementations of cultural processes cannot succeed unless they draw on this knowledge. There are simply too many degrees of freedom in human cultural behavior to allow its essence to be extracted from even the largest dataset. What is needed is for these degrees of

freedom to be reduced in such a way that noise can be maximally subtracted from signal. The sophisticated models of culture that are to be found in the humanities and social sciences allow exactly this, to the extent that they are the outcome of expert human judgment in critical interaction with other forms of expert human judgment.

If this is true, then it is a truth that announces the urgent need to bring these worlds together. By pairing bottom-up pattern recognition with top-down normative models, algorithms will become capable of modeling how human beings *actually* engage with culture. The result will be sophisticated forms of learning and prediction that are sensitive to the hidden cultural rules that every human being knows intuitively. This is the point at which the algorithms in the cloud begin to converge with the algorithms in your brain.

Texture AI is one of the companies leading this enterprise. We match deep knowledge of human culture and language with expertise in algorithmic learning. Our goal is to develop the metrics and models needed to represent human culture in its full depth. This is ambitious, but the rewards of success are high. Imagine

a world where culture – where *human* culture – is no longer the prerogative of humans. Imagine a world where algorithms are no longer just an amplified reflection of every bad instinct human beings possess. That's the world Texture AI wants to help build.

What's not to like about that?

Texture.

Regulating the Disrupters

JEAN TIROLE
Nobel Laureate Economist

The leading tech giants – such as Apple, Amazon, Facebook, and Google – explicitly set out to disrupt much of the world's industrial and social *status quo.* They have now succeeded (I suspect) beyond their own wildest dreams, and probably beyond what some of their founders would have wished, considering the baneful effects that social media have had on democratic elections.

Given the scale and scope of these firms' impact on our societies, it is no surprise that they inspire both hope and fear in the public consciousness. But one thing is clear: A small cohort of technology firms now guards the door to the modern economy.

That today's information-technology markets are highly concentrated is beyond dispute. In most cases, a single company dominates a given market. There is nothing abnormal about this, as users are prone to flocking to just one or two platforms, depending on the service. But there are still legitimate grounds for concern about whether competition is functioning properly.

Network Defects

There are two reasons why digital markets are so concentrated. The first is a network externality: We need to be on the same network as the person with whom we want to interact. That is Facebook's business model, and no one can doubt its success, at least insofar as the company's interests are concerned. If our friends are on Facebook, we need to be there, too, even if we would really prefer another social network.

When the telephone was invented, competition among (non-interconnected) networks in every country with a phone system ended with a monopoly. Again, this was not abnormal. Users wanted to be able to call one another easily, so they naturally congregated on a single platform. When competition was reintroduced into the telephone industry in the 1980s and 1990s, it was necessary that the networks be interconnected, so that a user on one had access to them all. Without regulation, incumbent operators would

not have granted such access to new, smaller entrants. While it is cheaper and easier to patronize several social networks (to "multihome") than multiple phone companies, it still requires coordination.

Network externalities can be direct, as in Facebook's case, or indirect, as in the case of platforms for which many apps or games have been created. The more users there are on the platform, the more apps there will be, and vice versa. In other cases, the volume of users may determine the quality of the service, by allowing for better crowdsourced predictions. This is how both Google's search engine and the navigation app Waze work. While competing search engines can match Google's results for the most common queries, they do not have access to enough data to do so for more unusual search requests. Moreover, new services often require data, which users of existing services supply.

Thus, users on the dominant digital platforms benefit from the presence of other users on the same platform, even if there is no direct interaction among them. The same is true for city dwellers. Though they are almost all strangers to one another, the presence of other city dwellers means more employment opportunities and easier job mobility – not to mention more bars, cinemas, and other amenities – than in less densely populated locations.

A Problem of Scale

The second reason for the high level of concentration in digital markets is that the dominant firms benefit from economies of scale. Some services require large technological investments, and if that service is a search engine, then

> **The online economy follows a winner-takes-all logic, albeit with different winners across sectors and time.**

> **Policymakers and regulators around the world must face the fact that the reasoning behind traditional competition measures is no longer valid.**

designing it will cost roughly the same regardless of whether it attracts two thousand or two trillion search requests per year. What will not be the same is the value of the user data that is generated. The search engine that receives two trillion requests can charge advertisers far more, and scale up far more quickly.

Hence, by dint of network effects and economies of scale, the digital economy almost inexorably creates "natural monopolies." The online economy follows a winner-takes-all logic, albeit with different winners across sectors and time. The Internet browser market was dominated first by Netscape Navigator, then by Microsoft's Internet Explorer, and now by Google Chrome.

There are exceptions, of course. Economies of scale and network externalities have not played a paramount role in the markets for digital music and movies, where there are a number of platforms, including Amazon Prime, Apple's iTunes, Deezer, Spotify, Pandora, and Netflix. But these services are differentiated by their degree of interaction with the user.

Adapting Policy to New Business Models

Policymakers and regulators around the world must face the fact that the reasoning behind traditional competition measures is no longer valid. It is now common for a platform like Google or Facebook to set very low prices – or provide a service for free – on one side of the market and very high prices on the other side. This naturally creates suspicion among competition authorities. In traditional markets, such practices could well be regarded as a form of market predation that is meant to weaken or kill off a smaller competitor. By the same token, a very high price on the other side of the market could mean that monopoly power has been brought to bear.

And yet, even small digital firms and start-ups now practice this kind of asymmetric pricing: consider, for example, free online newspapers that are funded wholly by advertising. Two-sided markets are prevalent in the digital economy, and a regulator who does not adequately

1:
FACEBOOK CEO MARK ZUCKERBERG TESTIFYING BEFORE A JOINT HEARING OF THE US SENATE'S COMMERCE AND JUDICIARY COMMITTEES.

2:
MARGRETHE VESTAGER, EU COMPETITION COMMISSIONER.

account for this unusual business model could incorrectly declare low pricing to be predatory, or high pricing to be excessive, even though such price structures have also been adopted by the smallest platforms entering the market. Regulators, then, will need to refrain from mechanically applying traditional principles of competition policy. When it comes to multi-sided platforms, these principles simply are not applicable in many cases.

New guidelines for adapting competition policy to two-sided markets would require that both sides of the market be considered together, rather than analyzed independently, as competition authorities still sometimes do. This will require care and a new analytical approach. But that is better than misapplying traditional principles or simply treating these sectors as legal no-go zones for competition authorities.

Rethinking Regulation

More broadly, there are four clear areas for regulation in the digital economy: competition, labor law, privacy, and taxation.

When one company has a dominant position, there is a serious risk that high prices and a lack of innovation will follow. A new enterprise that is more efficient or more innovative than an established monopoly must be permitted to enter the market; or, in the economic jargon, the market in question must be "contestable." If vigorous competition between companies at a discrete point in time is not possible, then we must at least allow for dynamic competition, in which a once-dominant firm is replaced by an upstart that has superior technology or commercial strategy.

New entrants into online markets often begin with a niche product; if it proves successful, they expand to offer a much wider range of products and services. Google began with only its search engine before it became the company we know today; Amazon started by selling books.

So what matters is whether new entrants can access the market in the first place. If a newcomer has a single original product that is better than what the incumbent offers, the incumbent might want to block it from gaining even a partial foothold in the market. The incumbent will do so not to improve its short-term profits, but to prevent the newcomer from later

competing in areas where the incumbent occupies a monopoly position, or to stop the newcomer from allying with the dominant firm's competitors.

This is why "tie-in sales" are a particularly pernicious anticompetitive practice. By requiring purchasers of one of its products to also buy a suite of other products, a monopoly firm can deny market access to new entrants across a range of areas. And yet it is impossible to formulate a one-size-fits-all policy for this problem. Whether competition authorities should forbid a dominant company from using tie-in sales or similar gambits (loyalty rebates, for example) will depend on their motive and rationale.

At the end of the day, the only valid way to ensure productive competition in the digital sector is to approach these questions on a case-by-case basis. Regulators must deploy rigorous analysis, and they must do so with alacrity to keep up with the pace of change.

The Pursuit of the Buyout

Complicating the competition picture further is the natural incentive new market entrants have to sell themselves to the dominant firm. This incentive ➜

is so strong that new entrants may be motivated more by the desire to extract monopoly rent from the incumbent than by an interest in delivering a new or superior service to the consumer.

But preventing such behavior is easier said than done. Antitrust law, especially in the US, requires authorities to bring evidence that a merger would reduce competition and harm consumers. This is understandable, but such a standard makes it impossible to invalidate the many acquisitions that occur before any real competition has actually taken place, such as Facebook's acquisition of the platforms WhatsApp and Instagram. Given this, the effectiveness of antitrust law ultimately depends on competition authorities' competency and neutrality.

Ad Hoc Antitrust

With rapidly changing technologies and globalization, traditional regulatory tools have become less effective, causing competition policy to lag. Breaking up monopolies or regulating public utilities requires identifying a stable competitive bottleneck or essential facility (the counterpart of the local loop in telecoms, the tracks and station for railroads, or the transmission grid for electricity). Regulation demands detailed accounting in a world of global companies without any supranational regulator. And it requires following firms over their lifecycles to measure the profitability of capital – an impossible task.

We must develop more agile policies, such as business review letters (giving limited legal certainty to firms for a practice, subject to conditions set by the authorities) or regulatory sandboxes where new business models can be tested in a "safe" environment. Regulators and economists must be humble; they will learn by doing, and their policies should not be cast in stone.

Work-Gig Balance

As for labor law, it is clear that current approaches are ill-suited for the digital age. Most labor codes in the developed world were conceived decades ago with factory workers in mind. As such, they give little attention to fixed-term labor contracts, and still less to teleworkers, independent contractors, freelancers, or students and retirees working part-time as Uber drivers.

We need to move from a culture focused on monitoring workers' presence to one focused on workers' results. This is already the case for many salaried employees, especially professionals, whose physical presence in a workplace is becoming a secondary consideration – and whose effort is, in any case, hard to monitor.

When confronted with current labor-market trends, legislators often try to fit new forms of employment into existing boxes. Is an Uber driver an "employee" or not? Some people say yes, because a driver is not free to negotiate prices, and is subject to various training requirements and vehicle specifications, including cleanliness. Perhaps most important, Uber reserves the right to terminate drivers with poor ratings.

Others argue that Uber drivers are not employees. After all, they are free to decide when, where, and how much they work. Some drivers derive all of their income from their Uber activity; others may drive for other ride-hailing platforms, or may draw income from working part-time in a restaurant as well. And, like independent contractors, they bear their own economic risks.

Moreover, various restrictions also apply to many self-employed workers, who are limited in their freedom of choice by the need to protect a collective reputation – such as that of a profession or brand. In many countries, independent physicians are not employees, yet they cannot set their own prices, and they must follow specific rules or risk losing their accreditation. Even an independent winemaker must respect regional certification rules.

Unfortunately, while the status of Uber drivers and other platform workers is debatable, the debate is going nowhere. Any classification that we settle on will be arbitrary, and will no doubt be interpreted positively or negatively depending on one's personal prejudices or ideological predisposition toward new forms of work. At any rate, the debate loses sight of why we classify work in the first place: to provide for workers' wellbeing.

Looking ahead, the priority should be to ensure competitive neutrality: the dice must not be loaded in favor of either salaried employment or self-employment. The state must promote the health-care

> # "We should worry that we no longer seem to have the right to oblivion, a basic tenet of many legal systems."

and social-security rights of gig workers like, say, Uber drivers. At the same time, it should avoid policies that would make the digital platforms unviable, even if they are unfamiliar and disruptive.

Rescuing Privacy

Progress is also needed when it comes to stopping firms and governments from intruding in consumers' private lives. It is well – though not universally – known that these entities collect large amounts of information about us. Yet, even if we are aware of this, we often fail to recognize the true scale of these processes or their consequences.

For one thing, we have less control over what firms and governments collect than we may think. For example, a company acquires and stores information about us that is shared by others (through e-mails, photos, or social networks), without us ever using its platform or even the Internet. Platforms also underinvest in security, as they internalize the consequences of a breach for their profit but not fully those for their customers.

We should worry that we no longer seem to have the right to oblivion, a basic tenet of many legal systems. We should worry about the possible breakdown of health-care solidarity, and the disclosure of potentially sensitive information about us (religion, politics, sexuality) in divisive domains. And we should worry about far-reaching state surveillance.

The European Union's General Data Protection Regulation amounts to only a small first step toward protecting us from such threats. Further steps should include the creation of a set of standardized policies that everyone understands (state regulation is consistent with "libertarian paternalism").

Keeping the Lights On

Lastly, because the Internet has no borders (which is generally a good thing), countries will increasingly need to cooperate on taxation, both to prevent tax competition and simply to derive some revenues from a huge swath of the economy. To that end, the 2015 agreement within the European Union to end tax competition on online purchases offers a promising model.

Specifically, the EU policy authorizes a purchaser's country to apply its value-added tax to any online purchase, whereas the previous regime levied the tax on the supplier. The result is that companies have less incentive to locate in countries with low VAT rates, or to seek out consumers in countries with high VAT rates.

The new system has proven to be a satisfactory regulatory response for business models such as that of Amazon, which bills the individual consumer. But it does not resolve the problem of platforms like Google, which technically does not sell anything to individual British, Danish, French, or German consumers, but rather charges the advertisers who do. Regulators across developed economies are discussing this problem, because the tax base in Google's case is much less clear than in the case of book or music sales.

All told, digitization represents a marvelous opportunity for our societies; but it also introduces new dangers, while amplifying others. To achieve an economics for the common good in this new world, we will have to address a wide range of challenges, from public trust and social solidarity to the ownership of data and the effects of technological diffusion. Success will depend, in particular, on whether we can develop viable new approaches to antitrust, labor law, privacy, and taxation. PS

Jean Tirole, the 2014 Nobel laureate in economics, is Chairman of the Toulouse School of Economics and the Institute for Advanced Study in Toulouse. His most recent book is Economics for the Common Good.

> ## The opportunities and challenges posed by financial innovation are clear. The policy responses must address both.

cost some of them their jobs. Individuals might gain as consumers, but lose as employees. The balance of these two effects will differ across segments of society, potentially leading to greater economic inequality.

And, as for crypto-assets, it is hard to see any benefit in them at all. They lack the basic properties of money, are prone to volatile valuations and manipulation, and are extraordinarily energy-intensive. Their opacity raises consumer- and investor-protection issues and opens the door for tax evasion and money laundering. Moreover, crypto-assets have been piggybacking on the trust that the traditional financial system has earned over the course of many years. A loss of confidence in crypto-assets could thus erode confidence in the broader financial system.

To contain the risks associated with innovation, policymakers, regulators, and supervisors will need to be as creative, nimble, and tech-savvy as the new players. They should consider creating innovation hubs to bring entrepreneurs and incumbents together, as well as "regulatory sandboxes" that allow innovators to test new technologies and products in a safe environment. Either measure would help policymakers stay informed about the evolving landscape.

To prevent regulatory arbitrage, rule-makers should follow the maxim of "same risk, same regulation." Entities vying for similar customers or offering similar financial services must follow the same rules regardless of where they are based. Setting clear regulatory boundaries reduces uncertainty and the risk that innovators will move into the shadows. But prudential authorities must also monitor financial institutions' exposure to companies and products that fall outside the regulated perimeter – a task that will require new sources of knowledge and data.

In the crypto world, "same risk, same regulation" means that companies raising funds through "initial coin offerings" should face the same standards and scrutiny as those offering shares. Likewise, the big tech companies should not enjoy an undue advantage when it comes to data access and sharing. Existing data-privacy codes have too many loopholes for unethical practices, and thus need to be reformed. The European Union's General Data Protection Regulation represents a step in the right direction. The question that policymakers need to keep in mind is how much privacy one should give up in order to access financial services.

Because innovation knows no boundaries, "same risk, same regulation" must also apply across countries. Domestic and international coordination among prudential, legal, tax, accounting, and telecommunications authorities is essential. Governments must also anticipate the impact of innovation on users and workers, not least by introducing training programs so that people will have the skills needed to keep up with the pace of change.

The opportunities and challenges posed by financial innovation are clear. The policy responses must address both.

Agustín Carstens, *Governor of the Bank of Mexico from 2010 to 2017, is General Manager of the Bank for International Settlements.*

1:
A TECHNICIAN INSPECTS
A BITCOIN MINING FARM.

Disruption, Concentration, and the New Economy

RAGHURAM G. RAJAN
*Former Governor of the
Reserve Bank of India*

The growing dominance of leading technology firms has occasioned an intense debate about the tradeoffs between efficiency and market power, while raising questions about what the changing structure of markets will mean for innovation and the distribution of wealth in the future. The annual Jackson Hole Economic Policy Symposium in Wyoming, organized by the Federal Reserve Bank of Kansas City, offered an excellent set of papers and commentators on the subject.

With respect to efficiency and competition, there is already cause for concern. John Haltiwanger of the University of Maryland has shown that the entry rate of new firms into the market has fallen sharply, particularly over the past 12 years; and Jay Ritter of the University of Florida has demonstrated a similarly steep decline in annual initial public offerings.

These findings suggest that young firms are increasingly agreeing to be acquired, rather than trying to grow into large public firms. At the same time, exit rates within many industries have remained relatively flat despite an increase in productivity dispersion. In other words, weaker producers aren't being knocked out of the market, implying a lack of dynamism in many sectors of the economy.

Meanwhile, measures of market concentration, such as the share of sales by the four largest firms, are up in a variety of industries in the United States, though it is not yet clear what conclusions one should draw from this. There is some debate over whether concentration is also rising in Europe, where somewhat tighter antitrust policies are in place. If it is not, then antitrust policies could explain the difference between Europe and the US in this regard.

Likewise, corporate profitability seems to be higher in the US than in Europe; but, again, it is not clear what that means. Some see it as a sign of increased monopolization in US industries. Others see it as a sign that dominant US superstar firms are innovating more, and reaping the benefits of higher productivity. But if that is the case, one must still confront the reality of low overall productivity growth worldwide. If innovation is so high, why is productivity growth still so low?

Concentrated Disruption

Before we get to that question, let us look at what we know. Current research suggests that rising concentration is a reflection not of market power, but of a shift in market share toward better-managed, more innovative firms – the firms that attract the best employees. Having congregated in a few superstar firms, the capable have become super-capable.

This would seem to be a good thing, insofar as it suggests that firms are gaining market share by becoming more efficient, and not simply by snatching up other firms while antitrust authorities stand aside. One would expect market concentration/monopolization to lead to higher prices, but there isn't much evidence of that happening. Of course, firms could be improving efficiency without passing on the savings, in which case even flat prices would be a source for concern.

Another development is the growing importance of "intangibles" such as software and intellectual property, which Nicolas Crouzet and Janice C. Eberly of Northwestern University suggest could be driving an increase in market concentration. Moreover, distinguishing among industries, they show that higher concentration is correlated with rising productivity in some sectors, and with growing market power in others. In consumer-facing industries where Crouzet and Eberly have found productivity gains, Alberto F. Cavallo of the Harvard Business School suggests that consumers have benefited in the form of lower prices. The broader point is that we cannot say definitively that rising concentration has been harmful to consumers.

Still, the health-care sector offers a cautionary tale. It, too, is heavily concentrated, but dominant firms seem to be intent on squeezing consumers, and they don't all demonstrate high levels of productivity. The question, then, is whether today's highly productive superstars in other sectors will eventually go down the same path. After all, while well-known market leaders such as Facebook and Google have been offering many products and services for free (which obviously benefits consumers), their business models have raised a number of pressing questions.

For example, one must consider whether the exchange of personal data for the use of such services constitutes a fair trade. There is also the matter of whom these companies do charge for services, and whether those costs (say, for the advertisements you are forced to watch) are being passed back to consumers.

It remains to be seen if the current arrangement – whereby users get free services in exchange for viewing advertisements and relinquishing data, firms pay platforms to access these ➡

> **Perhaps the biggest worry of all is the deceleration of technological diffusion.**

customers, and the platforms get a huge network of customers in exchange for their innovative services – will last. More important, there is the as-yet-unanswered question of whether it will preserve dynamism in these markets over the long term.

FAANGs Out

The next important question is whether the structure of key industries is slowing down investment, research and development, or the diffusion of innovation from superstar firms. Most economists would say that innovation is driven largely by competition, both within an industry and further afield, as well as by the threat of future competition. So, even if one is not too worried about the effects of concentration on innovation today, one still must consider whether that could pose a threat to future dynamism.

Here, I think there is reason to worry, given the falling rate of new market entries and the growing tendency among younger firms to be bought out. More often than not, such acquisitions are primarily

used by dominant firms to shut down or assimilate new products that might pose a competitive challenge in the future. There is plenty of evidence of this happening in the pharmaceutical industry; but we also know that the FAANGs (Facebook, Amazon, Apple, Netflix, and Google) will resort to such measures as needed.

In addition to stifling competition, this practice is also discouraging financing by venture capitalists, who now talk of a "kill zone" surrounding the major technology firms' main products. At this point, VCs are hesitant to finance anything that falls in the kill zone, because there is no prospect for growth there – only one-and-done acquisitions.

Another major advantage for dominant players is the ability to monopolize access to customers, or to leverage customer data. In a study of one million credit-card offers, Hong Ru and Antoinette Schoar of MIT have shown that companies may be exploiting data-driven insights into individuals' behavior to extract rents from them. Another obvious advantage for today's market leaders is the lock-in

1.

created by network effects, which tend to produce winner-takes-all outcomes.

In light of these incumbency advantages, we may no longer see as much competition as we did in the recent past, when firms were still vying for market share in key sectors of the economy. A related concern is one that Adam Smith raised 250 years ago. As the total number of firms decreases, there will be a greater risk of tacit or even explicit collusion, both *vis-à-vis* customers and in markets for labor and intermediary goods.

Perhaps the biggest worry of all is the deceleration of technological diffusion. Current data suggest that new ideas are not spreading from superstar firms to the rest of the economy. While some firms show strong productivity growth, and the dispersion of productivity within industries is increasing, we are also seeing lower productivity growth overall. There are a number of possible reasons for low diffusion, from intellectual property (IP) protections to constraints on labor mobility between firms. But whatever the cause, it is clear that we should be worrying even more about the future of productivity than its present.

The Lumpen Majority

A final concern is inequality. At the risk of oversimplifying, we have reached a point where the highest earners are concentrated in a few firms, with the rest largely lacking such earning opportunities. In other words, it is not the few at the top in every firm who are earning outsize wages, but instead the many in a few superstar firms. The question is whether that should make us feel better.

Obviously, neither scenario is very appealing. The more the top-skilled people congregate in a select few superstar firms, the more those left behind will wonder why the "elites" keep getting away with everything. It hardly seems fair that those reaping the lion's share of the rewards also happen to be so concentrated in a few companies on the coasts, rather than distributed more broadly across firms, sectors, and regions.

As for those left behind, Alan B. Krueger of Princeton University has warned that a variant of Smith's problem, namely collusion among a few firms in the labor market, has become increasingly salient. In certain markets, at least, we may be witnessing the rise of monopsonies (a single buyer), rather than monopolies (a single seller). In the case of the labor market, a company that enjoys a monopsony position – or that has implicitly colluded with other firms – can put downward pressure on wages across the board.

Krueger suspects that while monopsony power "has probably always existed in labor markets … the forces that traditionally counterbalanced [it] … have eroded in recent decades." At the same time that union membership has fallen, companies have increasingly engaged in practices that weaken workers' bargaining power – from non-compete clauses to the third-party staffing of companies. ➡

2.

3.

> **Central banking is hard enough as it is. It is harder still when there are politicians trying to score political points by attacking you.**

What Is to Be Done?

Having surveyed the data on market concentration, innovation, and the distribution of incomes, we should now turn to the policy implications of these trends. To my mind, policymakers should be particularly worried about how the behavior of superstar firms today could affect competition in their industries tomorrow. Politicians and regulators should take a hard look at whether IP and proprietary agglomerations of data are being used to stifle competition or prevent the diffusion of new knowledge and technologies across sectors. And they should consider policy instruments that go beyond the scope of traditional antitrust.

For example, some have suggested that individuals should have a right to their data. This could potentially improve diffusion, because firms would become purchasers of data, rather than sellers. No longer tied to any one platform, individuals could distribute their data to competing firms. Policymakers could also start to push for more interoperability between platforms, which would limit how much users could be tied to any particular structure.

In terms of labor, policymakers could intervene in a number of ways. For example, there might be a case for antitrust action against "non-compete" contracts, which essentially impose restraints on trade (of labor, in this case). Similarly, action could be taken to diminish the power of occupational-licensing regimes (such as for beauticians or plumbers), which tend to be dominated by the very people who have the greatest interest in protectionism. Why should those who already hold a given license be the ones to set licensing rules? One would think that a more neutral body should determine the extent of occupational licensing.

Central Bankers' Unenviable Task

At any rate, one of the most important effects of the economy's ongoing structural changes has been on the political economy of central banking. Fear of technological change, the declining quality of jobs, and the disruptions caused by superstar firms have given people plenty of reasons to be unhappy. Despite low unemployment, many workers are unhappy. They are stuck in non-superstar firms, where they harbor a general post-Great Recession resentment against elites and their policy agenda.

And, of all elites, central bankers seem to have the most strikes against them. Most have doctorates and speak in a language that nobody else understands. The quintessential "citizens of nowhere," they meet periodically behind closed doors in faraway Basel, where they discuss global financial conditions and the systemic effects of monetary policies. What they do not talk about, many believe, is Main Street, except when it factors into discussions about inflation.

No wonder there has been such a decline in public trust. It is bad enough when average citizens can scarcely understand the complicated tradeoff between inflation and unemployment. It is worse when one adds in public grievances over Wall Street bailouts and the perception that central bankers are focused on global conditions instead of domestic concerns. Yes, it is every central banker's job to think about such things; but that job is increasingly being met with suspicion by those who aren't in the room.

Central banking is hard enough as it is. It is harder still when there are politicians trying to score political points by attacking you. One should not envy central bankers as they navigate today's environment of distrust and derision, which itself is a product of the larger structural changes occurring in the economy.

Can central bankers win back the public's confidence, maintain global economic stability, and find ways to accommodate widespread technological disruptions all at the same time? That will be a key question in 2019 – and beyond. **PS**

***Raghuram G. Rajan**, Governor of the Reserve Bank of India from 2013 to 2016, is Professor of Finance at the University of Chicago Booth School of Business.*

How American Poverty Became "Fake News"

ANGUS DEATON
Nobel Laureate Economist

Under the administration of the incontinently mendacious President Donald J. Trump, everyone should worry about the integrity of America's official statistics. They should worry about much more under Trump, particularly the fate of democracy in the United States. But without credible official data, there can be no genuine accountability – and thus no democracy.

Consider the Trump administration's reporting on poverty in the US. It seems that the baseline numbers produced by the US Census Bureau are (so far) intact, but there has been a flurry of misinterpretations that go beyond the usual partisan spin.

Commentators on the right like to quote Ronald Reagan's 1988 claim that in the War on Poverty, declared by Lyndon B. Johnson in 1964, poverty won. That claim, perennially used as a cudgel to beat the social safety net that was expanded under Johnson's "Great Society" reforms, is consistent with official poverty estimates, the methodology of which has not been updated since the 1960s.

Because that methodology ignores taxes (including the earned income tax credit) and programs like food stamps (now called the Supplemental Nutrition Assistance Program, or SNAP), their effects are not counted, no matter how successful they are in reducing want. Such a widely acknowledged statistical flaw invites commentators to fill the hole with their prejudices, as Reagan did.

More recently, Trump's Council of Economic Advisers, in a July report arguing for work requirements to be attached to social benefits, claimed that, thanks to the American safety net, the War on Poverty "is largely over and is a success." This argument hinges on abandoning traditional metrics, which measure *income*, and switching to *consumption*.

Consumption is arguably (but only arguably) superior to income as a welfare measure, but it is unclear how many of the very poor participate in a burdensome and intrusive survey that has a 40% non-response rate. More worrying still is the

> 66
> **The result makes for dreadful reading. Documenting the extraordinary depths of poverty in parts of the US.**
> 99

> **Many of us believe that, because the US social safety net is so imperfect, extreme poverty is more prevalent there than elsewhere.**

essentially arbitrary "correction" to the consumer price index (CPI) that reduces the poverty line so that there are fewer people beneath it.

Perhaps the official CPI does not adequately capture quality improvements in goods and services. The consequences of this have been addressed in the scholarly literature, notably by a National Academy of Sciences panel that argued *against* a mechanical correction. But debating that issue is very different from abandoning the official CPI in favor of a more politically advantageous one that comes close to eliminating poverty.

A more egregious case of data manipulation concerns a report by the United Nations Special Rapporteur on extreme poverty and human rights. At the invitation of the US government, the Special Rapporteur, Philip Alston, examined extreme poverty in the US. He reported his findings to the UN Human Rights Council in June 2018.

The result makes for dreadful reading. Documenting the extraordinary depths of poverty in parts of the US, the report includes tent camps on the streets of Los Angeles, yards awash in untreated sewage because local authorities refuse to supply services, and the widespread use of fines and confiscations levied on poor people that many towns and cities are using to finance themselves. Whereas Johnson declared a war on poverty, parts of America are now waging a war on the poor.

Many of us believe that, because the US social safety net is so imperfect, extreme poverty is more prevalent there than elsewhere – and certainly among developed countries. Welfare reform that encouraged work has been good for some of the poor, but bad for the poorest, expanding inequality within the poor population and hurting the worst off.

Books by Kathryn J. Edin and H. Luke Shaefer and by Matthew Desmond have documented in detail the miseries of life at the bottom in America, and Shaefer and Edin argue that several million children in the US are living on less than two dollars a day. In a *New York Times* commentary

1.

1:
ANGUS DEATON.

2:
POVERTY IN THE LOWER
MISSISSIPPI DELTA.

published in January 2018, I noted that the World Bank now publishes estimates of global poverty that include the rich countries, and that those estimates show 5.3 million people in the US living on less than the equivalent of the world's global poverty line.

In my argument, I used $4 per person per day for rich countries as roughly equivalent to the global poverty line of $2 used for poor countries. There are more "globally poor" people in the US than in Sierra Leone or Nepal, and the poverty *rates* in the US and China are similar, despite the more than threefold difference in *per capita* income.

The World Bank's calculations that I reported were widely denounced – by both the right and the left. The Heritage Foundation argues that if one uses consumption, not income, there are only 250,000 globally poor people in the US. Never mind whether the parents selling their children's social security numbers to survive, or risking their children's safety to find a place to live, have time to participate in the consumption survey. Many on the left, meanwhile, refuse to believe that any American is as poor as the poorest in Africa or Asia. Whereas the right wants to decrease domestic

transfers, the left wants to increase foreign transfers.

The story then turns surreal. Alston's report drew an angry rebuke from the US ambassador to the UN, Nikki Haley, who claimed that "it is patently ridiculous for the United Nations to examine poverty in America," and an official US response saying that Alston's numbers were wrong. Yet the only numbers Alston used came from the US Census Bureau, an estimate described in the response as "the exaggerated figure cited by the Special Rapporteur." The response then approvingly cited the Heritage calculations, which are based on *my* $4-per-day poverty line.

And then, perhaps only coincidentally, the Trump administration pulled the US out of the Human Rights Council, with the result that Haley did not attend the report's presentation. She, like the Council of Economic Advisers, noted that the Trump administration knows how to tackle deep poverty, which is to force people to work.

That may or may not be true, but denouncing the Census Bureau's estimates in favor of those from the Heritage Foundation (there is evidence that agency

officials objected) or conveniently tampering with the CPI, and then treating the alternative numbers as superior to the official statistics, is surely well beyond the pale. Trump's administration showed in 2018 that it will admit no blemishes, whether extreme poverty or the unconscionable death toll following Hurricane Maria in Puerto Rico. And there is no reason to believe that further distortions of the truth, and the threat to democracy that such behavior implies, will not appear in the coming year. PS

Angus Deaton, the 2015 Nobel laureate in economics, is Professor of Economics and International Affairs Emeritus at Princeton University's Woodrow Wilson School of Public and International Affairs. He is the author of The Great Escape: Health, Wealth, and the Origins of Inequality.

Doing Business in the Great Disruption

MARK CLIFFE
*Chief Economist
of the ING Group*

How should companies respond to the Great Disruption? When surveying the global backlash against the economic and political *status quo*, they must recognize that it is in part directed at them. Populists and nationalists see business, or at least "big business," as part of the problem. Understanding the forces behind the Great Disruption, then, will be critical for companies hoping to survive and thrive in 2019 and beyond.

A decade ago, the global financial crisis cast a spotlight directly on financial institutions; but that scrutiny has since morphed into a more general skepticism about corporate behavior. While the tech giants that are driving the digital disruption have become the center of attention, no company should assume that the Great Disruption will be a mere passing storm. A prudent outlook would accept that today's polarization could get worse before it gets better.

After all, populists have been on the march in the midst of a sustained economic upswing and falling unemployment. Just think what will happen when the next recession arrives. Though forecasters are not ringing alarm bells about a recession in 2019, high asset prices leave financial markets vulnerable to destabilizing setbacks. And while the current crop of populists might not fare well in the next recession, they could well be replaced by others with even more radical ideas.

Moreover, while politicians come and go, other key elements of the Great Disruption will endure. The new-technology genie is out of the bottle. The rapid deployment of digitalization and artificial intelligence (AI) will be hard to stop, owing not only to the pervasive benefits these technologies

bring, but also to the competition they have spurred between countries – led by the United States and China – to be the winner that takes all.

Similarly, the environmental challenges of climate change and resource usage are not about to go away. If anything, they will intensify as a result of populist climate denial, delay, and prevarication.

Accordingly, companies should think of themselves as polar explorers, whose top priority is always to avoid freezing to death. To survive the Great Disruption, companies first need to be careful what they say. Policy advocacy risks triggering a backlash and boycotts, and one critical presidential tweet can send share prices tumbling. In an era of social media and fake news, active but sensitive reputation management is more challenging than ever.

Second, recognizing that trust in big business is fragile, corporate leaders need to understand not just populist politicians but also the motivations and desires of the people who support them. Foreign companies, in particular, must be attuned to local cultural diversity. And ensuring the privacy and security of client data is another critical ingredient in building and maintaining trust.

> **Already, policymakers in Europe and elsewhere have begun to look for ways to address the dominance of US and Chinese tech companies.**

Third, companies need to be better prepared to weather shocks, by de-risking their operations and balance sheets. Scenario and contingency planning, along with stress testing, are crucial for building the resilience and flexibility needed for survival. In particular, complex international supply chains and lean inventory-management techniques can be caught out by capricious political decisions and other shocks.

Once companies have built up resilience, they can start to look for opportunities that the Great Disruption may offer. To that end, multinationals should start behaving more like "multi-locals." With countries so internally divided, companies will need to pay more attention to the nuances of local interests when serving their customers. Looking beyond urban elites, there are profitable opportunities in catering to less advantaged segments of the population. These cohorts' concerns are what governments – populist or not – are under increasing pressure to address.

Moreover, digital technologies and AI are creating new possibilities to serve disadvantaged groups with segmented and personalized products. Already, policymakers in Europe and elsewhere have begun to look for ways to address the dominance of US and Chinese tech companies. If that increased attention leads to tax, data, and privacy policies that level the competitive playing field, there could be new business opportunities for others.

Companies also should consider adopting a "barbell" investment strategy: having made their core businesses resilient to polarization, they can reserve a small proportion of their investment budgets for bets that promise high pay-offs. This calls for agility, because companies will need to respond quickly to changing circumstances. But so long as they keep bigger buffers and reserves, they will be able to pounce on bargains after negative shocks.

Today's stretched asset valuations suggest that such shocks are becoming more likely. But even if they don't materialize in 2019, companies can start thinking through their options. A major focus in the months and years ahead will be the tension between the US and China, which may depress asset prices, presenting attractive entry points for the booming Chinese and intra-Asian regional markets.

Finally, companies should play the long game on environmental sustainability. Populism and nationalism may be weakening cooperation on these global challenges, particularly now that President Donald Trump has withdrawn the US from the Paris climate agreement. But this means that there will be an even greater need for action in the long run.

Alternatively, the populists themselves may come to see the attraction of shifting taxation from workers – especially their core voters – toward fossil fuels. This may not be imminent in the US, where Trump has committed to propping up the coal industry. But the falling cost of renewable energy presents a longer-term opportunity to make the shift away from fossil fuels. Not only will less expensive renewables depress fossil-fuel prices, but, absent policy action, they will also stimulate a counterproductive rise in energy consumption. To prevent this, policymakers could raise taxes on energy generally and use the revenue to fund cuts in other taxes.

None of this is to suggest that the corporate journey through the Great Disruption will be a comfortable one. It will be fraught with challenges, and not all companies will survive. But by understanding the sources of today's political polarization, companies can at least minimize the risk of being disrupted out of existence.

Mark Cliffe is Chief Economist and Head of Global Research of the ING Group.

Cooperation for a New Age of Volatility

SRI MULYANI INDRAWATI
*Indonesian Minister
of Finance*

Managing an economy is not for the faint of heart. Policymakers must constantly monitor the ever-evolving global economic landscape, and anticipate lightning-fast changes that can breed volatility and uncertainty. As today's political and economic turbulence attests, the impact of events in one place can be felt far and wide, but particularly in emerging economies.

To stay ahead of the curve, policymakers must put international cooperation above short-term national interest. And yet, in the last two years, protectionism, policy divergence, and a lack of coordination have begun to pose serious downside risks to the global economy. A confluence of factors is creating a perfect economic storm.

For starters, the US Federal Reserve has tightened liquidity through its interest-rate hikes, while the US Treasury's pro-cyclical expansionary policy (tax cuts and increased spending) has bolstered aggregate demand and pushed up the yield on ten-year Treasury bonds. Moreover, US trade policy *vis-à-vis* China and Europe has dampened global trade. As a result of this policy mix, the US dollar is appreciating, and capital flows into emerging economies are declining.

For countries like Indonesia, the danger now is that a full-blown US-China trade war could derail much of the socioeconomic progress that has been made in recent years. For decades, emerging economies have been tapping into international trade to boost growth and reduce poverty. Now, we must ask ourselves if this beneficial cycle is coming to an end. ➡

1:
SRI MULYANI INDRAWATI.

1:
SCENES OF DESTRUCTION FOLLOWING
INDONESIA'S DEADLY TSUNAMI.

At a time when we are facing rising global threats, relations among the advanced economies are more strained than they have been in decades, and this has given rise to a number of new problems.

Given that emerging economies are already integrated into global supply chains, these countries' policymakers must be more proactive in shaping the trade architecture and advocating for a global rules-based system. To maintain growth and stability amid volatility, they should focus on strengthening economic fundamentals, rather than on pursuing unsustainable quick wins. Even short-term issues should be addressed with a longer-term strategy in mind.

Above all, emerging economies need to find a common voice. Escalating rivalries threaten to make navigating the headwinds they face impossible. During the global financial crisis ten years ago, policymakers from around the world had the political courage to pursue collective measures that staved off a global depression. There is no reason why the response should be any different now.

In fact, the international community came together to speak with a single voice as recently as 2015, with the conclusion of the Paris climate agreement and the Sustainable Development Goals for 2030. The SDGs were developed through a truly collaborative effort, one that embodied its participants' optimism that poverty can be almost eliminated within our lifetime,

and that all people can partake in the fruits of growth and prosperity.

A mere three years later, that optimism is difficult to sustain. The idea of the world speaking with one voice seems like ancient history. Cooperation has been replaced by zero-sum unilateralism, and political leaders have become increasingly preoccupied with myopic, pro-cyclical, and populist policies at home. Even if their objective is to correct legitimate imbalances, policymakers must remember that rebalancing can have far-reaching spillover effects, especially when such adjustments bypass global rules.

In October 2018, Indonesia hosted the International Monetary Fund-World Bank Group Annual Meetings in Bali, where fiscal and monetary authorities from 189 countries converged to discuss many of the issues alluded to here. There was overwhelming agreement that the spirit of multilateralism must be kept alive.

In his plenary address in Bali, Indonesian President Joko Widodo (known as Jokowi) summed up the mood when he emphasized the need to shift from confrontation to cooperation. When global powers are preoccupied with competing among themselves, they fail to see looming threats that will affect us all.

2.

It is pointless to become the biggest power in a global economy that is sinking.

At a time when we are facing rising global threats, relations among the advanced economies are more strained than they have been in decades, and this has given rise to a number of new problems. As Jokowi has observed, today's great-power struggles look like something out of the popular HBO series "Game of Thrones." Consumed by rivalry, each "Great House" is oblivious to the shared existential threat from the north. We in the real world must not make the same mistake.

Indonesia learned much from the 1997-1998 Asian financial crisis and the collapse of 2008: namely, that we must remain focused on reforms and global cooperation. Hence, over the past two decades, Indonesia has undertaken important changes to strengthen its economic resilience and ensure that the economy is managed more prudently. As a result, the broad picture of Indonesia's economy is still bright, even with dark clouds gathering over the global terrain.

In anticipation of a potentially long period of global volatility, the Indonesian government will continue to strengthen its policy mix in cooperation with other authorities – domestically and across

1:
INDONESIAN PRESIDENT
JOKO WIDODO.

2:
ENGINEERS IN THE TUNNELS
OF JAKARTA'S MRT
CONSTRUCTION PROJECT.

national jurisdictions. At the same time, we will continue to build a stronger economic foundation upon which to sustain the momentum of growth, and to safeguard the poorest and most vulnerable in our society. At a time of deepening global uncertainty, we must focus on the common good – and pursue it together. **PS**

*Sri Mulyani Indrawati is the
Finance Minister of Indonesia
and Chair of the World Bank
Group's Development Committee.*

AFRI HIST PIVO

CÉLESTIN MONGA
Vice President and Chief Economist of the African Development Bank Group

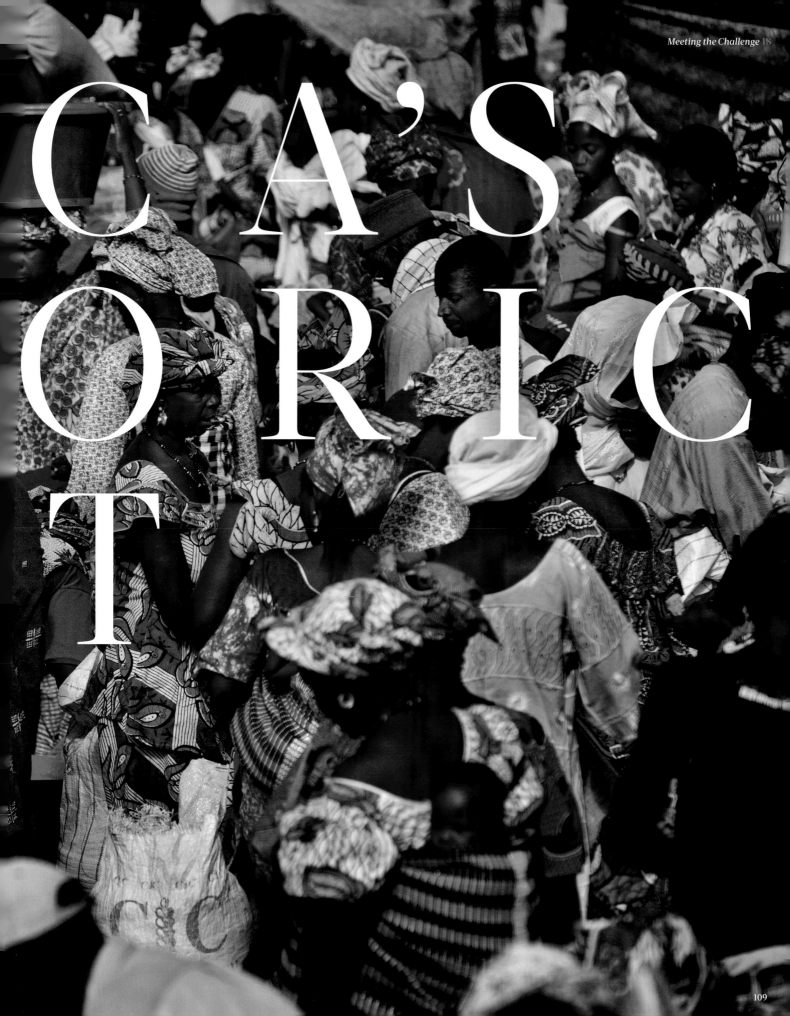

CA'S
ORIC
T

The year 2018 was marked by tremendous economic and political turbulence around the world. And yet, for future historians, it may well be the year when Africa started to claim its intellectual and economic-policy independence.

The unlikely trigger for what could turn out to be a continent-wide strategic shift was Rwanda's decision to increase tariffs on imported secondhand clothes and footwear in support of its local garment industry. This provoked an immediate hostile response from the United States, which suspended duty-free status for Rwandan textile exports under the African Growth and Opportunity Act (AGOA), America's flagship trade legislation for the continent.

For a small, landlocked African country that relies heavily on trade, this was a big deal. But the fact that Rwanda held its ground confirmed that times have changed. If Rwanda is willing to risk preferential access to the US market in order to develop its domestic garment industry, then it must be confident that it will find alternative markets for its exports.

Meanwhile, other African countries have also adopted a more independent attitude *vis-à-vis* the major trading powers. African governments have increasingly been taking a stand on a wide range of potentially controversial issues, including trade policy in East Africa, land redistribution in Southern Africa, and macroeconomic and debt-management policies in North Africa.

African governments' motive for stepping up now is not only economic; it is also about dignity, intellectual freedom, and a willingness to risk charting one's own course. And, more broadly, African leaders recognize that the ongoing transformation of the global economy means that no country will have enough power to impose its strategic preferences on others, even when they are much smaller, as in the case of Rwanda and the US.

Empirical research from the World Economic Forum (WEF) shows that tariff reductions and market access have become much less relevant for economic growth than was the case a generation ago. Trade is no longer about manufacturing a product in one country and selling it elsewhere; rather, it is about cooperating across borders and time zones to minimize production costs and maximize market coverage.

The WEF estimates that, "Reducing supply chain barriers to trade could increase [global] GDP up to six times more than removing tariffs." If all countries could bring the performance of border

administration, together with transport and communications infrastructure, up to just half the level of global best practice, global GDP would grow by $2.6 trillion (4.7%), and total exports would increase by $1.6 trillion (14.5%). By comparison, the complete elimination of all tariffs worldwide would boost global GDP by only $400 billion (0.7%), and exports by $1.1 trillion (10.1%).

Clearly, global value chains are now the dominant framework for trade. And, as we have seen, African countries such as Rwanda (as well as Ethiopia and Morocco) are already taking advantage of this paradigm shift. Rather than wasting time in unproductive policy discussions over tariffs, they are redirecting their strategies to focus on trade facilitation.

True, today's trade wars have disrupted international supply chains, and will continue to do so. But new constraints will also stimulate creativity and innovation. For example, as Meghnad Desai of the London School of Economics points out, "In the light of advances in technologies such as 3D printing and artificial intelligence, it is not far-fetched to imagine that businesses could manufacture domestically the intermediate products that they currently import." In this case, trade would continue apace, "but the product mix would shift from intermediate to final products."

Moreover, in an increasingly multipolar world, low-income countries will not have to rely solely on the West for financing and policy ideas (though they will have to be mindful of the risks of indebtedness and precarious governance frameworks). Even as global commerce has undergone a tectonic shift, traditional development thinking, policies, and practices have not.

Meanwhile, as the major emerging economies pursue technological and industrial development to escape the "middle-income trap," they are altering the distribution of roles and responsibilities across the global production system. Owing to the economic success of countries such as China, Vietnam, and Indonesia, other low-income economies in Africa and elsewhere now have substantial opportunities to boost employment in labor-intensive industries. After all, China now produces many of the high-value-added goods that once were the exclusive preserve of advanced economies.

1.

$1.6 TRILLION

IMPROVING BORDER ADMINISTRATION, TOGETHER WITH TRANSPORT AND COMMUNICATIONS INFRASTRUCTURE, TO HALF THE LEVEL OF GLOBAL BEST PRACTICE WOULD INCREASE EXPORTS BY $1.6 TRILLION.

$1.1 TRILLION

ELIMINATION OF ALL TARIFFS WORLDWIDE WOULD BOOST GLOBAL EXPORTS BY $1.1 TRILLION.

As China and others continue climbing the industrial and technological ladder, the necessary relocation of large parts of their supply chains to lower-cost countries will affect the costing and pricing of goods and labor everywhere. But developing countries can actually use their latecomer status to reap substantial economic benefits. Despite the wildly exaggerated threat of automation, African countries, in particular, can exploit their lower factor costs to promote successful labor-intensive industries in which they have a comparative advantage.

For example, African countries can lower the cost of doing business by building strategically located production clusters and industrial parks (including for green industries). They are also in a strong position to attract foreign direct investment, which brings the positive externalities of technology and know-how transfer, managerial best practices, state-of-the-art learning, and access to large global markets.

If managed properly, this two-pronged approach could provide ample employment for a low-skilled labor force, while rapidly increasing fiscal revenues. And this, in turn, would allow for improvements to infrastructure in other areas, thus creating the conditions for long-term prosperity and social stability.

While trade agreements such as the AGOA are still very important to African countries, broader economic and technological changes are opening up new opportunities, and smart policymakers are seizing them. This is a pivotal moment in North-South relations. After centuries of being politically and intellectually tethered to advanced economies with little to show for it, Africa is striking out on a new path of self-affirmation.

In this quest for prosperity, African leaders and policymakers have proved ready to withstand sanctions, threats, and setbacks. They may not all have read Nietzsche, but they know that what "does not kill us, makes us stronger." PS

1:
CÉLESTIN MONGA.

2:
VOLKSWAGEN'S ASSEMBLY PLANT IN KIGALI, RWANDA.

Célestin Monga is Vice President and Chief Economist of the African Development Bank Group.

THE GREAT RECONSTRUCTION

I f the "Great Disruption" of 2018 is to be overcome, the world will need a new framework for global cooperation. After World War II, the international community came together to design a set of institutional structures that facilitated collaboration in pursuit of a shared future. Now, it must do so again.

KLAUS SCHWAB
Founder and Executive Chairman of the World Economic Forum

This time, however, the challenge is not just geopolitical and economic. We are experiencing a fundamental change in how individuals and societies relate to each other. And by understanding this change, we can positively influence its outcome.

The first thing to recognize is that we are living through the Fourth Industrial Revolution (4IR) in which businesses, economies, societies, and politics are being fundamentally transformed. Since first conceptualizing the idea for the World Economic Forum's annual meeting in 2016, I have been clear: tinkering with our existing processes and institutions simply will not do. Instead, we need to redesign them so that we can capitalize on the abundance of new opportunities that await us, while avoiding the kind of disruptions that we are witnessing today. If we wait or rely on quick fixes to repair the deficiencies of outdated systems, the forces of change will naturally bypass these systems and develop their own momentum and rules.

The 4IR is already transforming our economic systems in a number of ways. For starters, the physical world is being dwarfed by a new digital, interconnected, integrated, and virtual world with a circular and shared economy. Manufacturing is being revolutionized by automation, localization, and individualization – all of which will make traditional supply chains obsolete. Competition is becoming less cost-based and is driven more by functionality and innovation. Soon, economies of scale will no longer provide the advantages they once did. The most precious resource will be talent, not traditional capital.

The 4IR is also putting unprecedented power and resources into the hands of just a few corporations. Today's leading digital firms are reshaping people's daily lives and disrupting traditional social patterns in ways a traditional business never could. From here on out, the mastery of artificial intelligence (AI) and big data, and the ability to operate massive platforms through the leadership of intelligent systems, will determine both corporate and national power.

At the same time, employment and income patterns will be transformed by the diffusion of AI-driven automation. Jobs will increasingly be self-created through innovative ecosystems. Traditional labor income will be replaced by accrued returns from creative tasks, venture capital, and first-mover advantage.

Already, global economic interactions can no longer be compartmentalized into the trade of goods and services, financial transactions, and investments. All economic flows are integrated into a comprehensive system of cross-border tangible and non-tangible value exchange. Rather than taxing labor, governments will have to start taxing the platform monopolies and mechanisms of value creation that are rooted in the cloud.

In the years ahead, national budgets will increasingly be strained by outlays for the hard and soft infrastructure needed to provide ecosystems for innovation and labor reskilling and upskilling, as well as social programs to support workers through the economic transition that is underway. A key priority must be to adapt education to the demands of the 4IR. Emphasis must be placed on nourishing creativity, critical thinking, digital literacy, and a capacity for empathy, sensitivity, and collaboration – all of which are necessary for ensuring that technology remains subordinated to ➡

1.

our needs, rather than the other way around. Moreover, education systems will have to be geared more for lifelong learning, both through digital delivery and face-to-face personalized development and coaching.

Beyond education, policymaking in general will have to adapt to the speed of change in the 4IR. New collaborative, agile governance models will have to be developed to avoid a scenario in which government policies continuously lag behind the technological frontier.

How countries respond to all of these changes will determine their future growth trajectories and positions on the world stage, to say nothing of their citizens' quality of life. As a process of borderless interconnection, the 4IR requires that national policies be integrated into a global system. Today, globalization is defined by the expansion of multilateral and bilateral trade; but in the future, it will describe the interconnectivity of national digital systems and the related flow of ideas and services.

Although many countries are still trying to catch up to the previous industrial revolutions, they should recognize that the 4IR offers unique opportunities for

leapfrogging to the newest innovations. Having reaped the benefits of the First Industrial Revolution, the United Kingdom became the dominant global power in the nineteenth century. It was succeeded by the United States, which, more than any country, took ownership over the Second and Third Industrial Revolutions. These three revolutions divided the world into industrialized and developing countries, with China declining in significance after having been a leading power for many centuries.

Today, the global balance of power is being redistributed again – and at incredible speed. Now that a single individual has the means to cause enormous destruction, we can no longer countenance a world divided between haves and have-nots. There is thus an urgent need for global cooperation and, at a more fundamental level, fresh thinking about what free, fair, and inclusive economic relations would actually look like in today's world.

We at the World Economic Forum will be starting that dialogue at our annual meeting in Davos in January 2019. As the foremost multi-stakeholder platform, the Forum has the ability and responsibility to drive this conversation forward, and, through our scientific and

1:
KLAUS SCHWAB.

2:
HUMANOID ROBOT SOPHIA DURING THE DISCOVERY EXHIBITION.

2.

> **Preparing for the 4IR will require sustained engagement and a broad consensus around actionable solutions.**

academic networks, to act as a catalyst for new ideas. Preparing for the 4IR will require sustained engagement and a broad consensus around actionable solutions. The Forum hopes to provide the "operating system" for this effort in the coming years, based on the conviction that, to be effective, these dialogues must be owned by all stakeholders – business, government, civil society, and the young. They must also focus on pursuing social cohesion, and, in today's fractured environment, will be most effective if driven by coordination rather than cooperation as a guiding principle.

Finally, we must recognize that these dialogues cannot be driven by a false dichotomy between global and national identities. We must embrace the individual, patriotic, and globalist identities as they exist in all of us.

After WWII, the international community laid the foundations for sustained peace, security, and prosperity. But the world has changed radically during the last seven decades, and it is time for a new approach. Only by embracing that challenge together can we shape our global future for the benefit of all. PS

The World's Opinion Page

Project Syndicate was established in the early 1990s as an initiative to assist newly independent media in post-communist Central and Eastern Europe. Expansion to Western Europe, Africa, Asia, and the Americas quickly followed, as publishers worldwide sought access to the views of leading thinkers and policymakers on the day's most important global issues.

1   *PROJECT SYNDICATE'S* NETWORK OF MEMBER PUBLICATIONS   13

1,264

WE DISTRIBUTED 1,264 COLUMNS IN 2017.

546

BY 546 CONTRIBUTORS.

156

IN 156 COUNTRIES.

21,596

IN 2017, PS COMMENTARIES WERE PUBLISHED 21,596 TIMES IN OUR MEMBER PUBLICATIONS.

Our rapid growth has been guided by rigorous editorial independence and a simple credo: all people – wherever they live, whatever their income, and whatever language they use – deserve equal access to the highest-quality analysis, from a broad range of perspectives, of the events, trends, and forces shaping their lives.

Project Syndicate thus provides an invaluable global public good: ensuring that news media in all countries, regardless of their financial and journalistic resources – and often in challenging political environments – can offer readers original, engaging, and thought-provoking commentary by the world's leading innovators in economics, politics, health, technology, and culture.

Without *Project Syndicate,* most of the publications we serve would be unable to secure comparable content. *Project Syndicate's* unparalleled range and caliber of opinion, our ability to provide analysis of breaking news, and our commitment to focusing minds on complex topics driving the news – development, Asia, Africa, and sustainability, among many others – now benefits some 300 million readers of more than 500 media outlets in 156 countries.